How to Heal
After
Narcissistic
Abuse

CAROLINE STRAWSON

How to Heal

After Narcissistic Abuse

A Practical Guide to **Dismantling Shame, Healing Trauma**, and **Thriving** After Toxic Relationships

HAY HOUSE

Carlsbad, California • New York City
London • Sydney • New Delhi

Published in the United Kingdom by:
Hay House UK Ltd, The Sixth Floor, Watson House, 54 Baker Street
London W1U 7BU
Tel: +44 (0)20 3927 7290; www.hayhouse.co.uk

Published in the United States of America by:
Hay House LLC, PO Box 5100, Carlsbad, CA 92018-5100
Tel: (1) 760 431 7695 or (800) 654 5126; www.hayhouse.com

Published in Australia by:
Hay House Australia Publishing Pty Ltd, 18/36 Ralph St, Alexandria NSW 2015
Tel: (61) 2 9669 4299; www.hayhouse.com.au

Published in India by:
Hay House Publishers (India) Pvt Ltd, Muskaan Complex, Plot No.3, B-2,
Vasant Kunj, New Delhi 110 070
Tel: (91) 11 4176 1620; www.hayhouse.co.in

A catalogue record for this book is available from the British Library.

Tradepaper ISBN: 978-1-4019-7610-1
E-book ISBN: 978-1-83782-109-9
Audiobook ISBN: 978-1-83782-108-2

This product uses responsibly sourced papers and/or recycled materials.
For more information, see www.hayhouse.co.uk.

10 9 8 7 6 5 4 3 2 1

Printed in the United States of America

This product uses responsibly sourced papers and/or recycled materials. For more information, see www.hayhouse.com.

In loving memory of Linda Patricia Hovland
June 24, 1941 – March 28, 2009

CONTENTS

Part III: Stepping into Your Best Self

LIST OF EXERCISES

INTRODUCTION

Welcome – I am so happy to have you here. This book is your narcissistic abuse healing bible; it's also the book I wish I had when I was healing. As you'll come to learn, I've been exactly where you are now and I know how hard it can be. Narcissistic abuse tests our resilience and inner strength and can shatter our world, leaving us feeling broken, lost, and alone. I too felt isolated for so long, and I want you to know that it doesn't have to be that way. Amidst this darkness, there exists a ray of hope – it *is* possible to take back your power and heal yourself. I'm living proof of that.

This book is about reclaiming ownership of your life, healing your inner child, and learning to thrive beyond narcissistic abuse. In these pages, I've integrated trauma-informed practices with positive psychology to support you in healing from trauma. Positive psychology is a branch of psychology that focuses on strengths, virtues, and factors that contribute to human flourishing. It provides a valuable framework for dismantling shame, building resilience, and living a fulfilling and meaningful life. Dr. Martin Seligman, a prominent psychologist, played a pivotal role in the founding of positive psychology and argued that psychology should not only be concerned with fixing what's wrong, but should also explore and promote what makes life worth living.[1] This makes so much sense to me as we live in a society that is sick and diseased, and I want to change that – this is why I integrate positive psychology into my trauma therapy. As a society, we look to just merely manage symptoms, but it's important to not just own your diagnosis, but to get curious and look at the root cause.

As we work through *How to Heal After Narcissistic Abuse* together, you'll learn:

- how to recognize the red flags of a narcissist

- why your nervous system is at the heart of your narcissistic abuse experience

- how your childhood has impacted your adult relationships

- how to identify your core emotional wounds

- how to release shame

- how to develop compassion and kindness toward your inner child – the most wounded younger part of you

- how to grow in strength and resilience using positive psychology

- how to live a trauma-informed life

- how to heal yourself and move from post-traumatic stress to post-traumatic growth

This book is your practical tool kit full of education, inspiration, and hope, with a heavy dose of humanness and compassion. It will not only help you to understand exactly what a narcissist is, but also what you need to do to start to not only survive, but thrive and flourish. By the end of this book, you will realize – just like I did – that you have the power to successfully process and integrate your experience into your own powerful story of personal growth and resilience.

When I work with my clients, we look at three time lines: the past, the present, and the future. In this book, I want to do the same with you, but taking it gently at first. We'll start by identifying exactly what a narcissist is and uncovering those red flags before carefully exploring how your past may have impacted your relationships and behaviors.

We'll then go a bit deeper, when you're ready, and look back at your childhood and start to identify any deep emotional wounds within you. We'll then start the healing process with some simple tools you can use to immediately ground and regulate your nervous system in the present as you are dealing with the devastating effects of narcissistic abuse.

Once you're able to regulate your nervous system and understand your past, we'll look at how narcissistic abuse can lead to a renewed sense of purpose, before finally exploring what I feel is the most exciting part of healing after narcissistic abuse – post-traumatic growth. This is a positive psychology term and a phenomenon where individuals not only recover from trauma, but emerge from it stronger and wiser. This is why this book is your lifeline because it not only gives you the hope and light of what is possible, but also shows *how* it's possible with all the exercises and interventions included throughout. Post-traumatic growth illuminates the potential for positive change and personal growth, even in the face of unimaginable adversity, which we know narcissistic abuse is. I certainly know that I've had post-traumatic growth and, while this may seem like an impossibility for you right now, if you commit to this book and yourself, you'll start to move toward this too.

I don't want you to just merely survive, I want you to live your best life and thrive.

My Story

In 1996, I met a man who I thought I was going to be with for the rest of my life. He swept me off my feet and made me feel so special with grand gestures – he even got a tattoo with my nickname 'Carrie' on his arm a few months after we met. I know you're probably shouting at the book right now, but he was filling a big hole in my soul, so I completely missed all the red flags. I didn't feel good enough and desperately wanted someone to see me, to hear me, and to validate me. As we'll come to see, these are all key attachment wounds.

When I was with my now ex-husband, I always felt like he was never quite present. Even on our wedding day, I questioned whether I was doing the right thing – my gut was telling me otherwise, but everyone was already at the wedding, and I just hoped getting married would make it better. It didn't. I never, ever truly felt connected to him, but I know now that was because he was incapable of showing love and emotion and being part of a healthy relationship.

When we had our son, I put everything into being a mother because this was the only time I felt a sense of worth. It was like my ex-husband and I were existing together, but not really married, so I just threw myself into motherhood, which I loved. I gave up my work, even though I was earning more, which is another red flag. Then, when we tried for another child, I kept miscarrying. In fact, I miscarried four times and I was devastated. It felt like I was now a failure as a mother, too. It really affected me and I felt unsupported. Then, by some miracle, I fell pregnant again with our daughter. But a nightmare was coming and at the worst time.

When I was six months pregnant with our daughter, I found out my ex-husband was cheating. He made the excuse that he had felt so helpless as I was going through four miscarriages, and this woman had been supporting him. So, what did I do? I comforted him and then I called her and comforted her too as she didn't know I was pregnant! From the moment we conceived my daughter to when we eventually split up nearly three years later, I never again let him touch me. I completely shut down and, when my daughter was born, I was diagnosed with depression and started taking antidepressants.

We went to marriage counseling for a while. This turned out to be a blessing because the therapist could see exactly what my husband was. In fact, this therapist was the one who told me to google 'narcissistic sociopath.'

In 2009, we were still together but living very separately (my ex-husband was cabin crew so was away a lot) when the worst thing ever happened to me – my mother, my rock, my safe place, died suddenly of a ruptured abdominal aortic aneurysm. It was like someone had pulled the rug from under me. Where was my safe place now? My dad had never been there for me emotionally and I had one sister in America and the other nearly two hours away.

My relationship with my husband was getting worse and, when I look back, I was too dissociated and a shell of myself to recognize it. I put on weight and wore gray baggy tracksuits, and would often drink wine and eat unhealthy food to numb myself.

My ex-husband started to stay away more and more, saying it was good to give us space. I knew he would be cheating, but I was so low, I didn't even care. I just wanted to be a mother to our children. Then, in August 2010, he told me he was leaving me. I knew this may not be true, but he told me that there was no one else and he just needed to be on his own. He asked me to tell our children, but I said no. I told him he needed to tell them. Our daughter was having a nap so he only told our son and, when he did, our son fell to the floor crying. Within five minutes, my ex-husband had left under the guise of not wanting to put me through any more pain as clearly I was unhappy – the classic false altruism of a narcissist.

On the Monday after he left, the nightmare truly began as I started to find out the state our finances were in. We were in over $90,000 worth of debt! I felt scared. I was now a single mother, with barely any income in a house with a big mortgage and no mother to help support me. My ex gave me the minimal amount he legally had to, as he took great pleasure in telling me. Eventually, he sent me a text that was clearly not for me, but it confirmed what I already knew – he was cheating again.

The abuse did not stop after he left. This is called post-separation abuse. Often, when you break up with a narcissist, it doesn't end and can actually escalate. Narcissists will frequently use money and the courts to perpetuate the abuse and sometimes this can feel even worse than the original relationship. The money coming in didn't meet the money going out and, each month, I was sinking further into debt, culminating in April 2013, when I was made homeless with my two children. It was one of the lowest points of my life. I felt so ashamed. How could my life be such a train wreck? When I turned 40 in June 2013, I remember sitting there feeling so angry that he had robbed me of the best years of my life and thinking that it was downhill forevermore. I felt like my life was over and, on many occasions, in the darkness, I thought about ending it all. But my children were my driving force and I couldn't leave them. I felt broken. I finally realized that I'd been in an abusive marriage – I'd been married to a covert narcissist and I didn't even see it. I felt so stupid and filled with shame.

I knew something had to change, even though I wasn't even sure how or whether I even had the energy. I came to realize that I'd been waiting and waiting for someone to come and rescue me, and I mean literally! Having grown up with fairy tales, I had this warped vision of my Prince Charming coming in on a white horse and sweeping me off my feet, making it all better. No one came. At the time, I felt like my family weren't even there, but I know now that this was all down to my expectations and childlike needs in wanting others to fix my life. I remember feeling so desperately alone – I could literally feel it in my bones. I just wanted someone to love me, to make it all better. When I realized that I was truly on my own in this world, it felt scary. My heart felt empty and numb. It really was the worst day of my life. But I had a glimmer of light inside of me and I hope this book ignites a similar glimmer in you. I realized that if no one was coming, I needed to do this myself. It felt liberating that I could let go of having to rely on anyone ever again, that actually I could rely on myself for everything I needed instead. If it was going to be, it had to be up to me. I had to stop looking for others to rescue me.

I started my own business in network marketing to try to earn some extra money and became one of the top business builders in the UK, which enabled me to pay off my debt. I was getting free holidays and bonus checks, but the work wasn't lighting me up. I came to see that what I loved was helping people. I realized that there was a huge lack of professionals who actually understood narcissism from a nervous system and trauma-informed perspective. There was so much shame and misunderstanding and I wanted to change that. So, with my medical background (I'd trained as a podiatrist), I left network marketing and started to retrain.

Just over 10 years after my husband left me, I created my School of Trauma-Informed Positive Psychology to educate, inspire, and teach individuals, workplaces, and schools all the things I wish I'd known around trauma-informed practice and positive psychology. I now have a podcast called *Trauma & Narcissism Redefined* with over 5 million downloads and a YouTube channel with over 2 million views. Me, Caroline — the woman who was at rock bottom! I still have to pinch myself.

I feel so blessed that I have this opportunity to share my darkest days to give you light and hope because you, too, can move from post-traumatic stress to post-traumatic growth with new beginnings and a brighter future.

How to Use This Book

Each of you reading this book will be at a different stage of your healing process — from only just realizing you have a narcissist in your life to having felt stuck for years. This book is your bible wherever you are at. My advice is to work through the whole book in order first because each and every chapter contains exercises and education for you to use and implement *now*. In addition, doing so will help you understand that this abuse is *not your fault* and that there's hope in living your best life again, or even for the very first time, whatever age you are. Once you've worked through the whole book, I would recommend that you keep going back to the chapters over and over again because you'll get different learnings each time. Remember that healing is not a magical destination – it's a lifelong journey and one that I'm on with you, right by your side.

Narcissistic abuse need not define our lives. It can become a catalyst for positive change. No matter where you are on your journey, it's my hope that all of you will come to see that experiencing narcissistic abuse can catapult you to leading an even happier, deeply joyful, and connected life. Personal growth is available to us all.

Please take as long as you need to go through the book. As you learn to listen to your body again, you'll come to understand that not all people are dangerous. We are wired for love and connection – and this is all within your reach.

I urge you not to just read this book; please action the exercises too, because if nothing changes, nothing changes. You deserve to heal, but for that to happen you have to take responsibility for your own healing and do the exercises I've included.

When you stay committed to each and every chapter and keep going through this book, not just once, but again and again, I truly believe that this will be your legacy. You are a cycle breaker, and you deserve a life of joy, love, and connection.

Healing from narcissistic abuse was the hardest thing I've ever had to do, but it was also the most empowering. Rediscovering my self-worth, confidence, and inner strength has been an incredible journey of self-discovery. Remember, you are not alone, and there is hope for a brighter future beyond the shadow of narcissistic abuse. You deserve to be in a relationship that uplifts and respects you.

As you'll come to learn in the chapters that follow, you can never change the narcissist, but you can change how you respond. The only thing stopping you from living the life I know you deserve is YOU, and this book will take you by the hand and start you on that journey.

Let's heal together.

PART I

Understanding Narcissistic Abuse

CHAPTER 1

The Dynamics of Narcissism

Before starting on the journey to healing, it's important for survivors to first understand narcissistic abuse and what a narcissist is. Truly understanding narcissism will open a beautiful portal for your healing and a deep knowledge of the pain that you are suffering, without losing your sense of presence and self. In this chapter, we'll reframe our understanding of narcissism, so we can approach it with compassion while still holding the narcissist accountable for their behavior.

What Is Narcissism?

A narcissist is officially defined as someone with a medical diagnosis of narcissistic personality disorder (NPD). However, I see this definition as flawed in several ways. We'll come on to why in just a moment, but first let's explore what the official traits of a narcissist are according to the *Diagnostic and Statistical Manual of Mental Disorders* (DSM), which professionals use to diagnose mental health disorders:[1]

1. A grandiose sense of self-importance, e.g., exaggerates achievements and talents, expects to be recognized as superior without commensurate achievements).

2. A preoccupation with fantasies of unlimited success, power, brilliance, beauty, or ideal love.

3. A belief that they are 'special' and unique, and can only be understood by, or should associate with, other special or high-status people (or institutions).

4. A need for excessive admiration.

5. A sense of entitlement, i.e., unreasonable expectations of especially favorable treatment or automatic compliance with their expectations.

6. Interpersonally exploitative behavior, i.e., takes advantage of others to achieve their own ends.

7. A lack of empathy, i.e., is unwilling to recognize or identify with the feelings and needs of others.

8. Envy of others or a belief that others are envious of them.

9. Arrogant and haughty behaviors or attitudes.

For an individual to actually get a diagnosis of NPD, they must display five or more of these traits. Now, I'm sure you're already starting to see the flaws here! Let's pretend that the narcissist in your life needs a diagnosis of this personality disorder. Firstly, to get any diagnosis, there needs to be a level of ownership and acceptance that something is actually wrong. I can hear you shouting at the book right now and I hear you. Narcissists will never take any responsibility or ownership for the hurt and destruction that they leave behind. Instead, it's always someone else's fault why they behave the way they do.

Secondly, let's say the narcissist does agree to go to a mental health professional because there's something 'off' in your relationship (as we'll come to see, this is often just lip service to keep you dangling just enough that you stay). They go to the appointment knowing that they're being put under scrutiny. How do you think they'll act? Will they act as they do with you and show off their full-blown narcissism so they can get a nice, neat diagnosis? (I can hear you shouting again.) No, of course they don't.

It's so rare for anyone to ever get a NPD diagnosis because narcissists take zero responsibility for their behavior – they see any issues as your fault. I remember going to marriage counselling once with my ex-husband and I came out of there so angry because he was playing the victim. He said that he had struggled with my four miscarriages and hated seeing me so sad, and that's why he had cheated on me while I was pregnant – so the counsellor ended up feeling sorry for him. That's how good narcissists are at giving people what they need to get them on side, and this makes it so hard for you. But you're in the right place – I believe you and you are not crazy.

I think it's so important to reenvision narcissism away from this medical diagnosis of NPD. In my mind, just because someone doesn't have a diagnosis, it doesn't mean that they're not a narcissist. If you have a cold, do you need a diagnosis to know it's a cold? If you have a headache, do you need a diagnosis to know it is a headache? You get the idea.

Just because the person in your life does not have a diagnosis, it does not mean they are not a narcissist.

My interpretation of narcissistic abuse and the way I approach it with my community is as a descriptive term for behaviors. Below are just some of the traits a narcissist may have:

- sense of entitlement

- grandiose sense of self-importance

- lack of empathy

- need for admiration

- arrogance

- manipulative, controlling behavior

- coercive control

- social isolation

- verbal abuse

- mood swings

- addiction

- gaslighting

- victim mentality

- blaming

- disregarding boundaries

If you recognize any of these typical traits, it might be that you're dealing with a narcissist. It's important to note that narcissistic abuse does not just happen in intimate partner relationships. Narcissists can be parents, siblings, children, friends, work colleagues, and even CEOs and politicians. Narcissism holds no bounds – anyone can be a narcissist, meaning that this can affect each and every one of us. I've lost count of the number of times I've spoken with someone who says they've never encountered a narcissist, and then, by the end of the conversation, they suddenly have this realization about someone in their life!

Though this book primarily focuses on the romantic relationships we can find ourselves in with a narcissist, this doesn't mean that it won't benefit you if you've experienced narcissistic abuse in other areas of your life. The knowledge about yourself that you'll come away with and the tools in this book are life-changing, whatever your situation.

THREE SIGNS YOU'RE DEALING WITH A NARCISSIST

1. You excuse their bad behavior

Narcissists don't take criticism lightly and you may find that you start to make excuses for them to friends and family, and offer reasons why they're behaving like they are, minimizing their behavior. You may try to improve a situation quietly and then let the narcissist take credit. You may find yourself saying things like, 'You don't know them like I do' or 'They're just tired.' You find yourself constantly trying to cover up their behavior. This is often a self-preservation mechanism because, if you don't make excuses, then you know their behavior will escalate once you're home and behind closed doors. To save face, a narcissist may appear to take bad news well publicly, but privately they can take out their anger and insecurities on the victim.

2. You're on edge all the time

You feel like you're walking on eggshells when you're around a narcissist, worrying that what you say or do may be taken out of context and you may then be yelled at or given the silent treatment. Every day when you wake up, you're trying to sense what type of mood they're in and hoping that today will be a good day. You might find yourself not wanting to look in the mirror, or wearing gray, black, or baggy clothes as you don't want to be visible. You feel like you're unable to take deep breaths and are constantly shallow breathing as your inner system feels the danger of your circumstances, and you can feel weak for staying engaged in the narcissistic relationship.

3. You jump between emotions and behaviors

Often you feel like you're angry and want to shout and scream at the narcissist to leave, or you want to just run away. Then, when you don't, you criticize yourself. You may feel like you're just existing and not living your life, and then, in the next moment, try to please and appease the narcissist in the hope that they'll minimize their behavior. This is an indication that you're jumping through the different states of the nervous system, which we'll explore in Chapter 4.

The Two Main Types of Narcissism

Narcissism is more than mere self-centeredness. It isn't just the person who walks into a room and commands attention. It's pervasive and insidious. Being abused by a narcissist isn't like flicking a light switch where one day they're nice and the next they're abusing you. It's slow and it chips away at the core of who you are without you even realizing it. This is what makes it so hard, because they do all of this behind closed doors – they have one face for the public and one for you.

I teach about 10 types of narcissism, but the two main umbrella terms are 'covert' and 'overt' – the rest sit under these two categories. This book focuses on both types, although covert narcissism is stealthier, and I believe more dangerous as it often goes undetected. It's important for you to know the signs of a narcissist so you know what you're dealing with and can help protect yourself.

Overt narcissism

An overt narcissist is someone who thinks they're incredibly special and important. They believe they're better than everyone else and want everyone to see them that way too. They love attention and will do things to get it, like bragging about themselves or showing off their achievements, even if they're not that amazing.

Overt narcissists often lack empathy. This means that they don't really understand or care about how other people feel. They might say or do things that hurt others without even realizing it. They also tend to be really good at manipulating people to get what they want. They might be very charming or use flattery to make others do things for them.

Overt narcissists also feel entitled; they think that they deserve special treatment and that the rules don't apply to them. If they don't get their way, they can get angry or upset. Despite their confident exterior, many overt narcissists actually have low self-esteem deep down. They use their big personality and bragging to hide their insecurities.

Having a relationship with an overt narcissist can be tough because they often put themselves first and don't consider how their actions affect others. They might come across as self-centered or demanding, making it hard for others to connect with them on a deeper level. I'm sure we can all think of a few overt narcissists in the public eye. Dealing with an overt narcissist means setting boundaries to protect yourself and taking care of your own well-being, as they may not prioritize your feelings or needs. We'll come to explore how you can do this in Part II.

Covert narcissism

Many of us think of a narcissist as the overt type we explored above – someone who demands the spotlight – but what about their elusive counterpart, the covert narcissist? Covert narcissists can be the most dangerous type of narcissist because their behavior is often difficult to recognize, leaving you feeling confused, frustrated, and trapped in the relationship.

Covert narcissists are skilled at tactics like manipulation, gaslighting, and emotional abuse. They can make you feel guilty, inferior, and responsible for their problems. They use charm and flattery to gain the trust and admiration of others, but ultimately their behavior is driven by a deep sense of entitlement and a lack of empathy. Covert narcissists are skilled at hiding their true nature behind a façade of vulnerability and victimhood. While overt narcissists may be loud and obnoxious, covert narcissists are more subtle in their manipulation and may appear charming or even empathetic.

Because covert narcissists can hide their true selves, you may not realize you're being abused until it's too late. Leaving the relationship is a struggle, as the covert narcissist convinces you that you are the problem, or you can't survive without them. This makes the covert narcissist particularly dangerous, as they can inflict lasting emotional harm on you without being detected. The covert narcissist's manipulation and control can lead to a slow erosion of your self-esteem and sense of reality.

Here are some reasons why spotting a covert narcissist is like finding a needle in a haystack:

- Covert narcissists are adept at masking their inflated sense of self-importance. They can convincingly act as the victim or the martyr, drawing sympathy and admiration from those around them.

- Unlike their overt counterparts, covert narcissists employ subtle manipulation tactics, often leaving you questioning your own judgment. Gaslighting and guilt-tripping are their weapons of choice.

- Covert narcissists have an uncanny ability to appear vulnerable, fragile, and emotionally sensitive. This draws caring souls like moths to a flame, making it challenging to believe they could be anything but genuine.

- Covert narcissists often criticize indirectly, disguised as constructive feedback or concern for your well-being. They undermine your self-esteem while appearing concerned for your growth.

- These individuals can switch between their charming, caring persona and their hidden narcissistic side in the blink of an eye. One moment, they're your biggest supporter; the next, they're undermining your achievements.

Understanding this hidden form of narcissism is crucial for protecting your mental and emotional well-being. By spotting these subtle manipulators, you can set boundaries, maintain your self-esteem, and distance yourself from toxic relationships. All the tools and techniques you'll learn throughout this book will enable you to heal from this type of narcissistic abuse.

The Narcissistic Abuse Cycle

Narcissists know how to manipulate and chip away at your self-esteem slowly but surely. They make you doubt your own perceptions and feelings, leaving you feeling like a mere shell of your former self. It's therefore crucial to recognize the signs of an abusive relationship. Constant criticism, controlling behavior, belittling, and a lack of empathy are all red flags. But sometimes, they're so subtle that it's tough to see them.

Narcissistic abuse typically follows a specific cycle, which is a four-stage pattern of behaviors: idealization, devaluation, discard, and reconciliation. This abuse cycle is a repetitive pattern used by narcissists to control you. It's like a roller coaster of tension, explosion, and temporary calm.

When tension builds, you can feel scared and anxious. Then, the narcissist explodes with abuse, making you feel trapped and helpless. Afterward, they act nice and apologize, giving you breadcrumbs of hope and keeping you attached to them.

This cycle tricks you into thinking that things might get better, making it hard for you to break free from the narcissist's power and control; you become accepting of the breadcrumbs of love.

It's very common for people to fail to recognize the manipulation tactics that narcissists employ at each stage of the cycle, so I've included the most common ones below.

Idealization

Narcissists are great at cognitively knowing just how much they need to do in order for you to stay with them. This is the first stage of the narcissistic abuse cycle, known as the idealization phase. In this phase, they will shower you with flattery, gifts, praise, approval, attention, and acts of perceived kindness – all acts that will fill the hole in your soul, 'hoover' you in, and give you hope that the relationship is OK. At this stage, there's a release of feel-good hormones, such as serotonin, dopamine, and oxytocin.

Love bombing

When you first start dating a narcissist, they may engage in a tactic called 'love bombing,' which is an intense form of flattery and affection that is designed to make you feel special and loved. Remember, my ex-husband got a tattoo of my name on his arm just three months into our relationship and, to me, it was a gesture saying, 'I love you and you are worthy.' But now, looking back, it was a big red flag.

While it's lovely to be nice to each other at the start of a relationship, you need to have clear boundaries. Healthy relationships take time to develop and require mutual respect, trust, and communication. If you feel uncomfortable or overwhelmed by the intensity of the attention and affection from a new partner, it's OK to take a step back and assess the situation. Trust your instincts and seek support from friends, family, and loved ones.

Devaluation

The next stage of the cycle – devaluation – happens when you don't change your behavior in alignment with how the narcissist wants you to. This is a huge trigger for them, so they need to punish you to exert that sense of power and shift it back to them. Devaluation can happen behind closed doors, when they are more covert and stealthier, but overt narcissists take no shame in devaluing in public. This can make everyone present feel uncomfortable and can therefore reinforce your shame as no one sticks up for you out of fear of the reaction of the narcissist.

In the devaluation phase, the narcissist flips their behavior, and you're faced with criticism, cruelty, disapproval, degradation, rejection, rage, and silent treatment. In response, you start to produce 'stress' hormones such as cortisol, epinephrine, and norepinephrine.

Gaslighting

One of the most insidious forms of manipulation in this stage of the cycle is gaslighting. A toxic person who gaslights might:

- not want to take your thoughts or concerns into account

- restructure or make up past events to shift the blame onto you

- insist you did things that you definitely know you didn't do

- tell others about your state of mind, behavior, or feelings

A narcissist who's gaslighting you might say that you're crazy, imagining things, or pass things off as just a joke. Signs of gaslighting can consist of blatant lying or constant cover-ups, denying that conversations or events ever happened, actions that contradict words, and broken promises.

When met with gaslighting, your self-esteem slowly erodes and you begin to question what is real, doubting reality. The narcissist may manipulate others to see you differently. When I came out of my marriage and had counselling, words like 'gaslighting' were said to me and I was shocked. I didn't know whether I believed it or not. That didn't happen to me… or did it? It was only when I started looking into what had happened that I realized I had lost myself.

Gaslighting is psychological abuse and leaves you feeling crazy, lacking in trust in yourself, and empty inside.

Gaslighting is a form of emotional abuse used by narcissists to make you feel like you're going crazy. YOU ARE NOT!

SIGNS OF PSYCHOLOGICAL ABUSE FROM THE NARCISSIST

Abuse does not always mean physical abuse and walking away from fights with bruises and broken bones. Just because you don't see the pain, it doesn't mean it's not there. Words can cause your inner body the same amount of damage as being physically abused. Psychological abuse can include:

- name-calling, criticizing, shaming, or humiliation
- constantly monitoring your activity or location
- dismissing or minimizing your feelings
- withholding attention or affection

- extreme jealousy over your time with friends and family
- overwhelming you with compliments or gifts to later manipulate you

If you stay with an abuser, you are not weak. You are not stupid. You are not at fault. You are abused. You are not alone. I see you and I am here to help guide you through your healing journey.

Discard

The next phase is known as the discard phase. During this phase, the narcissist employs various tactics to sever emotional ties and control you. They may become emotionally distant, withdraw affection, give you the silent treatment, or exhibit cruel behavior to diminish your self-esteem. Gaslighting and blame-shifting are common tools used to make you feel responsible for the abuse – that it's actually your fault. The narcissist might also seek new partners or interests, looking for what's known as more 'narcissistic supply' – the drug of choice for a narcissist – further isolating you. This phase can feel emotionally devastating, leaving you confused, hurt, and struggling with a profound sense of loss, abandonment, and rejection, perpetuating the cycle of abuse.

FLYING MONKEYS

Flying monkeys are people around the narcissist who will keep on feeding their narcissistic supply. They do this for one of two reasons. Firstly, they actually believe what the narcissist says as they're such a good liar and secondly, just like you used to, they're conforming to the narrative of the narcissist because the alternative may mean they get further bullying or abuse from them.

Smear campaigns

The goal of a smear campaign is to isolate you from your social circle, family, and friends, so you feel alone, vulnerable, and powerless. The reason narcissists do this is because they want to punish someone who has rejected them, so they tarnish your reputation and create a distraction from their own negative behavior.

Below are some tips to help you deal with a smear campaign:

- Document everything: If you're being targeted by a smear campaign, it's essential to document every incident, including who said what, when, and where.

- Don't engage with the narcissist: Narcissists thrive on attention and drama, and engaging with them will only make the situation worse.

- Seek support: A smear campaign can be isolating, so it's crucial to seek support from trusted family and friends, or join a support group (see *Resources, page 239*).

- Be proactive: If you suspect that a smear campaign is starting, take proactive steps to protect your reputation.

- Take legal action: If the smear campaign involves defamation or other illegal actions, you may need to take legal action to protect yourself. Speak to a lawyer who can advise you on the best course of action.

A smear campaign is emotionally and professionally damaging. However, by documenting everything, seeking support, and taking proactive steps to protect your reputation, you can weather the storm and come out stronger on the other side. Remember, a smear campaign reflects the narcissist's character, not yours, so don't let it define you.

Reconciliation

Sadly, the cycle of abuse does not end there, as narcissists then often 'hoover' their victims back into the relationship. Hoovering is a term we use with a narcissist to reference a form of emotional intimidation to suck you back into another cycle of abuse. When the narcissist feels that they're starting to lose control, they may go through a cycle of trying to make things better. They can suddenly change their behavior with romantic gestures or try to validate your feelings to regain power and control and 'hoover' you back in. Once you've been sucked back in, the cycle of abuse starts again.

The Effects of Narcissistic Abuse

One of the things victims of narcissistic abuse find the hardest is how they feel others see the narcissist. Narcissists are very different in public than they are in private. The narcissist will act like they're the victim, and you end up feeling invalidated because you see others taking sides with them.

When I look back at my experience of narcissistic abuse, I felt stifled. I was constantly putting on a mask and silencing my voice because I was so scared that people would think I was crazy and stupid. I kept silent for so long, afraid that people would judge me or not believe me. This insidious form of psychological abuse wears the victims down, so they start questioning themselves. Victims often feel angry, lost, alone, and like no one believes them.

Narcissistic abuse is a form of emotional and psychological trauma that can have a lasting impact on your mental health, sometimes leaving you with all the symptoms of complex post-traumatic stress disorder (C-PTSD) – a condition that can develop in response to ongoing trauma or abuse, which is exactly what being in a relationship with a narcissist leads to. Often it is characterized by a pattern of manipulative and controlling behavior, which can cause you to feel helpless and trapped. The chronic and repeated exposure to this abuse can lead to symptoms such as emotional dysregulation, anxiety, and depression.

Narcissistic abuse had such a huge effect on my mental health: I was suffering with C-PTSD, depression, anxiety, and self-harm. Each day I would be trying not to have a panic attack, living in a constant state of hypervigilance. That feeling of being lost and alone can seem like a long, dark tunnel with no light at the end of it. I thought my life was over and had such a deep feeling of rejection and abandonment that it felt like it was etched into my bones.

I would wake up each morning feeling groggy from using alcohol the night before to numb myself out, having not had good, restorative sleep, and my hands would be tingling with anxiety. My children would be asleep, and I would go into my bathroom and sit on the floor and cry. My breathing would become so rapid as I cried that it was a challenge to not dip into a panic attack; often I would fail. The self-harm was a way of focusing on physical pain rather than the emotional pain in my head that felt too much to bear. I was so filled with shame; I couldn't believe this was my life now.

I felt like I was never going to shake off this feeling of disgust at myself and thought that maybe it actually was all my fault. I even questioned whether I, myself, was the narcissist, which you may have done as well. By nature of you even considering this, let me reassure you, it means that you're not a narcissist as no narcissist would ever wonder if they were one.

Maybe this is your life now; maybe you also feel this way. I don't want your life to be like that because of narcissistic abuse for a second longer. You now have this book, and you deserve more.

Anxiety

One common effect of narcissistic abuse that many of my clients suffer with is anxiety. This doesn't just leave you hyperventilating and rocking back and forth; there can also be:

- random bursts of irritability

- obsessive behavior and nitpicking

- pacing

- silence

- hypersensitivity

- zoning out

Having suffered with anxiety myself, I can relate to ALL of these. If a trigger happened, I could feel myself down-spiraling and the anxiety starting. This is something I'm passionate about eradicating – the tools and strategies in this book will help you to learn to cope and then, in turn, minimize and eradicate anxiety from your life.

Emotional eating

This is another common coping mechanism for those who have experienced narcissistic abuse, as it can provide a temporary escape from painful emotions and feelings. Chronic stress, such as that experienced during narcissistic abuse, can also cause the body to release the stress hormone cortisol, leading to weight gain and difficulty losing weight. I massively struggled with my weight following narcissistic abuse, and felt ugly and filled with shame. If this is you, be kind to yourself because you are beautiful as you are right now.

Avoiding intimacy

It's important for you to understand that avoiding sex and intimacy is a common response to the trauma of narcissistic abuse. It's not a reflection of your worth or desirability and you are not frigid. After my ex had multiple affairs, I didn't want to be intimate with him as I saw this as dangerous.

Reactive abuse

Reactive abuse is when the narcissist deliberately manipulates a situation so that you'll react to make it look like you are, in fact, the abuser. YOU ARE NOT. This is a tactic used by the narcissist where they will 'poke the bear' — in other words, you — to get a reaction, and the bigger the better. You may shout, argue, or even get physical. They know exactly what buttons to push to get a reaction out of you. They may even record it so they can use it against you to try to intimidate you with sentences like, 'What would your family think if they could see this?' The narcissist is blame-shifting so they can use your behavior and recordings to show others a story that they have created about who you are.

The narcissist will try to act like they're the victim, and you end up feeling invalidated because you see others taking sides with them. People often see you as 'crazy' or dramatic. You seem unstable, imbalanced, and full of fear and doubt. You're angry, depressed, and sometimes lash out. You're experiencing overwhelming emotions and are probably wearing them on your sleeve for all to see. This can feel very frustrating because, if you react, you're then perpetuating what the narcissist is saying about you.

Narcissists will do whatever they can to avoid taking responsibility for their behaviors. This means if you're the victim and you're being abused, you might fling insults, scream, throw things at the abuser, or lash out at them. Let me repeat: You are not a bad person, you are being abused.

Be kind to yourself. Narcissistic abuse is ABUSE – it's trauma to the very core. Healing from the effects of narcissistic abuse can take time, but it is not a life sentence – it requires a holistic approach, including support groups, trauma-informed coaching, therapy, mindfulness and meditation, journaling and self-care, a lot of which we will explore in Part II. First, though, we need to delve further into understanding narcissistic abuse.

In my experience, one of the missing pieces when we look to heal from narcissistic abuse is the educational aspect and understanding ourselves and the nervous system. I've found that if we only work on the actual presenting issues, while this can help, having a deeper understanding of narcissism, and of our body and brain, sets us up for successful healing.

With this knowledge, we can then start to understand why we feel the way we do from a biological perspective and that it's not actually us being weak. This can be extremely validating. For me, this is the first step in your healing journey and, without it, it really slows down the healing process. In fact, in my opinion, this should be taught in schools. In the next chapter, we'll therefore start your journey of knowledge with understanding your attachment style and how this may have contributed to you attracting a narcissist into your life.

CHAPTER 2

Exploring Attachment Styles

The previous chapter may well have confirmed what you already suspected – that you're dealing with a narcissist. If so, I'm sure many of you, like I did, have wondered whether there is something wrong with you. Why do you keep attracting toxic people? I even realized that some of my friends over the years were also narcissists, but I had no idea at the time! So why was I such a magnet to a narcissist? Maybe you've asked yourself this question too.

In this chapter, we're going to explore this through the lens of attachment styles and how they can influence our relationships as adults.

Attachment Theory

Before we can move forward with our healing, it's crucial to recognize the role of attachment in our development. Attachment theory underscores the significance of early relationships with caregivers in shaping our emotional development. Secure attachment forms when caregivers consistently meet a child's emotional needs, creating a sense of safety and trust. However, inconsistent, neglectful, or abusive caregiving can lead to attachment wounds, leaving individuals with unresolved emotional scars. These attachment wounds often manifest in adulthood as insecure attachment styles like 'anxious,' 'avoidant,' and 'disorganized,' which we'll further explore in just a moment.

Developed in the mid-20th century from his work on the impact of maternal separation on children during and after World War II, John Bowlby proposed that a child's early experiences with their primary caregiver profoundly influence their emotional development and the ability to form healthy relationships throughout life.[1] Mary Ainsworth, a developmental psychologist, expanded upon this theory and conducted the groundbreaking 'Strange Situation' study, which provided empirical evidence for different attachment styles.[2] Her research laid the foundation for understanding how infants react to separation and reunion with their caregivers.

When it comes to healing from narcissistic abuse, a deep comprehension of attachment theory can be invaluable for several reasons:

- Understanding the roots of narcissistic abuse: Attachment theory helps us grasp why narcissistic abuse has such a profound impact. It emphasizes the significance of early attachment bonds with caregivers, and how disruptions or deficiencies in these bonds can lead to emotional vulnerabilities later in life. Individuals who experienced insecure or disorganized attachments in childhood are more susceptible to attracting narcissists, as they may seek validation and love from unhealthy sources.

- Recognizing patterns of attachment: Recognizing your own attachment style and that of the narcissist can shed light on the dynamics of the relationship. Narcissists often have avoidant or disorganized attachment styles, which can explain their need for control, manipulation, and the cycle of abuse that we explored in the last chapter. Understanding these patterns can help you disentangle yourself emotionally.

- Validation of feelings: Many survivors of narcissistic abuse struggle with self-blame and self-doubt. Attachment theory validates your emotional responses by explaining that the attachment system is biologically wired within us. You can understand that your feelings of fear, anxiety, and desperation are natural reactions to an unhealthy attachment bond. This validation can be empowering and promote self-compassion.

- Healing through secure attachments: Healing from narcissistic abuse often involves building healthier relationships. Attachment theory provides a road map for achieving this. It emphasizes the importance of secure attachments, which are characterized by trust, emotional availability, and empathy. By learning about secure attachment dynamics, you can work toward forming healthier connections in your life.

- Breaking the cycle: Attachment theory can help you break the cycle of abuse. When we have experienced narcissistic abuse, we may unconsciously repeat the same patterns in subsequent relationships. Understanding attachment dynamics can empower you to recognize red flags and make healthier choices in your relationships, reducing the likelihood of falling into abusive dynamics again.

- Trauma-informed healing: Attachment theory is closely related to trauma theory, as narcissistic abuse can be deeply traumatizing. A trauma-informed approach to healing acknowledges the impact of early attachment disruptions and helps you process your trauma in a compassionate and understanding way. This approach is more likely to lead to lasting healing and recovery.

- Therapeutic benefits: Attachment theory serves as a foundation for many attachment-based therapies, such as Internal Family Systems, which we'll explore in the next chapter. These therapies are designed to target the core attachment wounds and help you heal from the inside out, addressing the root causes of your pain.

Understanding attachment theory is vital when healing from the devastating effects of narcissistic abuse because it provides you with a comprehensive framework for understanding the origins of abuse, recognizing attachment patterns, validating your feelings, and guiding you toward healthier relationships and recovery.

By delving into attachment theory, you can embark on a journey of self-discovery and healing.

The stages of attachment

There are generally seven stages of attachment:[3]

1. Pre-attachment: birth to six weeks. Infants are instinctively social and seek proximity to caregivers. They don't display strong attachment preferences yet.

2. Attachment in the making: six weeks to eight months. Infants start to recognize familiar caregivers. They prefer certain caregivers, but can accept comfort from others. Trust and security are gradually established.

3. Classic secure attachment: eight to 24 months. Infants develop a strong attachment to their primary caregiver (usually their mother). They seek closeness, display separation anxiety, and rely on the caregiver as a secure base.

4. Attachment as a launching pad: 24 months to six years. Toddlers become more independent, but maintain a secure base in their caregiver. They explore the world and return for comfort and support when needed. The caregiver–child relationship becomes more mutual and reciprocal.

5. Mutual attachment: six to 12 years. Children continue to explore and develop autonomy. They trust their caregiver's availability and support. Attachment figures provide a safe haven for emotional regulation.

6. New attachment figures: six to seven years to puberty. Children start to consider their caregiver's perspective. They understand and accept separations for longer periods. The attachment relationship becomes more complex.

7. Adulthood: puberty onwards. The attachment system serves as a model for adult relationships. Securely attached individuals tend to have healthier, more stable relationships. Insecure attachment in childhood may lead to difficulties in forming intimate relationships.

These stages illustrate how attachment patterns formed in childhood can influence an individual's emotional and relational experiences throughout their life. Think of your phone: We'll often update our phone's internal operating system so it works on the best technology for efficiency. Our attachment to our parents and caregivers is like our internal operating system. This is fine, if we've been inputted with a secure operating system, but what if there are bugs and glitches that then become the baseline for our adult relationships? When was the last time you updated your internal operating system that was inputted during your childhood? Is that still the most effective for you?

Attachment theory helps explain the base and foundation of why we show up the way we do, and it can affect everything from our personal life to our professional life. This is why it's vital for us to understand so we can see that, again, this is not our fault and we're not weak. Just as a phone can get clunky and slow, we can get clunky in our relationships. We need to rewire our nervous system and input a new, up-to-date operating system.

Let's now take a closer look at the four main attachment styles.

The Four Attachment Styles

Attachment theory has identified four primary attachment styles:

Secure attachment

Presentation: Children with secure attachment styles tend to be confident in exploring their environment when their caregiver is present. They seek comfort and support when distressed, but readily return to exploration once reassured.

Impact on relationships: Adults with secure attachment styles typically have healthy, fulfilling relationships characterized by trust, effective communication, and emotional intimacy. They are comfortable with both autonomy and interdependence. Feels like nirvana – as you'll know, this is not the relationship with a narcissist!

Anxious attachment

Presentation: Children with anxious attachment styles are often clingy and anxious even when their caregiver is present. They may exhibit distress when separated but have difficulty calming down upon reunion.

Impact on relationships: Adults with this attachment style may struggle with excessive dependence on their partners, fear of abandonment, and heightened emotional reactions. They often seek constant reassurance and may experience intense jealousy. They'll be clingy and hate any type of conflict.

Avoidant attachment

Presentation: Children with avoidant attachment styles show independence and self-reliance. They may appear indifferent when separated from their caregiver and may not seek comfort upon reunion. They have learned it isn't coming anyway.

Impact on relationships: Adults with this attachment style may prioritize self-sufficiency and downplay the importance of emotional intimacy. They may have difficulty expressing their own emotions and empathizing with their partner's feelings. They'll have a strong flight response and being in a relationship with an avoidant attachment adult will seem like they're never quite present. Sound familiar?

Disorganized attachment

Presentation: Children with disorganized attachment styles display a mix of clinginess and avoidance. They may exhibit contradictory behaviors, such as approaching their caregiver while looking away, like they are testing the waters.

Impact on relationships: Adults with this attachment style often grapple with internal conflicts and ambivalence about intimacy. They may struggle with trust, frequently pushing away those they desire closeness with, making it challenging to maintain stable relationships.

As you can see, attachment styles formed in our early childhood can have profound effects on our adult relationships:

- Communication patterns: Our attachment style influences how we express our needs and emotions. Secure individuals tend to communicate openly and honestly, fostering healthy dialogue in relationships. Conversely, anxious and avoidant individuals may struggle with effective communication, leading to misunderstandings and conflicts.

- Conflict resolution: Attachment styles affect how people handle conflicts within relationships. Secure individuals are more likely to engage in constructive conflict resolution, while anxious individuals may become excessively distressed during disagreements, and avoidant individuals might avoid conflicts altogether.

- Trust and intimacy: Trust is a cornerstone of healthy relationships. Secure individuals find it easier to trust their partners, fostering emotional intimacy and mutual support. In contrast, anxious and avoidant individuals may struggle with trust issues, hindering the development of intimacy.

- Relationship satisfaction: Secure individuals often report higher levels of relationship satisfaction, as they're more likely to experience a sense of safety and comfort in their relationships. In contrast, anxious and avoidant individuals may face challenges that contribute to lower relationship satisfaction.

- Patterns of attraction: Attachment styles can influence who individuals are attracted to and who they form relationships with. For example, anxious individuals may be drawn to avoidant partners, creating a cycle of push–pull dynamics in relationships.

- Parenting styles: Attachment styles also influence how individuals parent their own children. Securely attached individuals tend to provide a nurturing and emotionally supportive environment for their children, whereas those with insecure attachment styles may struggle to meet their children's emotional needs.

Our attachment style is a learned behavior that comes from our caregivers. If a child has a parent who doesn't express love and emotion, this can leave the child feeling unloved. If their parent is behaving like this, the child will think it's their fault. This creates an anxious attachment style, meaning the child will feel anxious in relationships because they feel nothing is good enough so they'll keep moving toward the caregiver in the hope of receiving love.

On the flip side of this, the child could then become avoidant: 'What's the point in trying to be seen and heard as I never am anyway?' The perception is that relationships bring pain so they'll avoid and keep a distance as a child, which transcends into adulthood.

This can also bring about disorganized attachment, which I'm certain I had an element of: I wanted to get close to people but countered that by pushing them away because I was worried that I wouldn't be good enough.

When I look at my parents and their attachment styles, they were like a magnet to each other, just like I was a magnet to a narcissist. My mother was anxious and desperately wanted to be loved. This had come from her childhood experiences and her father, so she would overcompensate for this, and her sense of worth came from being a mother. In fact, she created the need in me to need her. Read that again as many of you may relate to this.

My father, on the other hand, was avoidant. He never showed love or emotion, and I was always scared of him shouting. His avoidant attachment felt to me that because he was distant, I needed to show him that I was good enough, as my interpretation was that he would then show love. I thought that he was choosing to withhold love because I wasn't good enough, but I didn't realize that he wasn't showing me love because he was, in fact, *incapable*. No one had taught him and his avoidant attachment was his coping mechanism.

My opinion is that most narcissists are avoidant. You never feel close enough to them, but, as we saw with the cycle of abuse in the previous chapter, they give you just enough breadcrumbs to stay. I always used to say to my ex-husband that he was in a different universe as I never felt fully connected to him. My perception of that, as it was a familiar feeling from my childhood, was that I needed to do more, be more, yet, as I moved forward, he would retreat. As a result, I felt totally alone. I was married to someone, but it felt like I was the loneliest woman on the planet and couldn't tell anyone. Narcissists can make you feel like this as they give you just enough to have hope and stay. As an anxious attachment, which most of us are in relationships with narcissists, this was devastating and a real trigger for all my core wounds.

Take the following quiz to see what your attachment style is.

ATTACHMENT STYLE QUIZ

For each of the questions below, choose the answer that best represents your feelings and behaviors in relationships. Tally your points at the end to determine your attachment style.

When my partner needs emotional support, I:

- Always provide support (1 point)

- Frequently provide support (2 points)

- Sometimes provide support (3 points)

- Rarely or never provide support (4 points)

I worry about my partner leaving me:

- Rarely or never (1 point)

- Sometimes (2 points)

- Frequently (3 points)

- Always (4 points)

I find it easy to trust my partner:

- Always (1 point)
- Most of the time (2 points)
- Sometimes (3 points)
- Rarely or never (4 points)

I prefer to keep some distance and independence in my relationships:

- Rarely or never (1 point)
- Sometimes (2 points)
- Frequently (3 points)
- Always (4 points)

When my partner seems distant, I:

- Don't get concerned and give them space (1 point)
- Feel a little worried but respect their space (2 points)
- Get anxious and try to get closer (3 points)
- Panic and become overly demanding of their attention (4 points)

I often fear rejection or abandonment:

- Rarely or never (1 point)
- Sometimes (2 points)
- Frequently (3 points)
- Always (4 points)

Expressing my needs and boundaries in relationships is:

- Easy and natural for me (1 point)

- Doable but sometimes challenging (2 points)

- Difficult for me, and I avoid it (3 points)

- Extremely hard, and I rarely express them (4 points)

I feel comfortable balancing emotional closeness and independence in my relationships:

- Always (1 point)

- Most of the time (2 points)

- Sometimes (3 points)

- Rarely or never (4 points)

My emotions in relationships are:

- Consistent and stable (1 point)

- Somewhat unpredictable (2 points)

- Often all over the place (3 points)

- Highly chaotic and unpredictable (4 points)

My history of relationships could be described as:

- Consistent and healthy (1 point)

- A mix of stable and turbulent (2 points)

- Often tumultuous (3 points)

- Chaotic and unpredictable (4 points)

Scoring

Add up the values next to each of your responses to each question:

- 10–20 points: secure attachment

- 21–30 points: anxious attachment

- 31–39 points: avoidant attachment

- 40 points: disorganized attachment

Interpretation

- Secure attachment: You are comfortable with both intimacy and independence in relationships. You trust your partner, express your emotions openly, and maintain healthy connections.

- Anxious attachment: You often worry about abandonment, seek reassurance in relationships, and may become anxious when your partner is distant.

- Avoidant attachment: You prioritize independence, struggle with emotional closeness and trust, and may have difficulty expressing your needs and boundaries.

- Disorganized attachment: A score of 40 indicates a disorganized attachment style, characterized by confusion, mixed emotions, and a history of unpredictable or chaotic relationships. This attachment style can be complex and may benefit from professional support for a deeper understanding.

It is important to note that attachment styles are not fixed for life. I can honestly say that I have probably experienced all four of these attachment styles. As I was on my healing journey, I found that I went from anxious to avoidant to disorganized to secure. That doesn't mean that every relationship in my life is secure, but I can now navigate them so much better.

Having this information about your attachment style provides a profound understanding of how your early emotional bonds shaped you and, consequently, your adult relationships and attraction of narcissists. Each attachment style presents unique patterns of behavior and emotional responses that impact communication, conflict resolution, trust, and relationship satisfaction. However, attachment styles are not set in stone, and by utilizing everything you'll learn in this book, you can start to recognize red flags in relationships and develop more secure attachment patterns, leading to healthier and more fulfilling relationships.

I know doing this work can bring up a huge amount of emotion and I want you to know that you are not alone. It can be hard exploring our attachment style as it takes us back to our childhood. You may know that you had a dysfunctional childhood, or you may be like me – I thought I had the perfect childhood when, in fact, my parents were both flawed human beings doing their best. This therefore impacted my attachment and led to an anxious attachment style.

The next chapter explores the impact of digging into our childhood and how trauma can affect our brain and body.

CHAPTER 3

It's Not Your Fault

As we saw in the last chapter, every single one of us will have an attachment style based on our childhood interpretation of our parents' or caregivers' behavior. Our attachment style is very individual – you can have siblings who had the same caregivers but have completely different attachment styles. This is why doing the work is so personal; it's a journey of self-discovery, and how you feel is how you feel. No one has walked in your shoes. Similarly, early traumatic experiences are unique, but can be damaging in so many ways.

Many trauma experts believe that most disorders listed in the *DSM* are really giving a label to symptoms that have all come from childhood trauma. When I say trauma, I don't mean just the big events that may happen to us, but our nervous system being overwhelmed with a person's behavior or an event. Trauma to each individual is trauma to them. It's not a spectrum of 'mine was worse than yours' or 'that wouldn't have affected me like that.'

As children, we're very egocentric and think the world revolves around us, meaning that, if anything bad happens, we feel it must be our fault. If our parents get a divorce, it must be because we're not worthy. If we're abused, it must be because we're not good enough. If a parent neglects us, it must be because we're unlovable. A child needs a reason, and that reason becomes themselves.

Going through my divorce forced me to really take a look back at my childhood. My mother was one of the most loving and maternal women I've ever known and, growing up, I thought she was the archetypal mother. She stayed at home, cooked, cleaned, and took me to school. But she had severe rheumatoid arthritis and I don't ever remember a time when she wasn't ill or in pain. She had a tough childhood, and her drive was her three daughters: me and my two older sisters. Her sense of worth came from being a mother and she was totally wrapped up in making sure we were educated and could always look after ourselves.

As the youngest, there was a huge amount of pressure on me when my sisters left home. I was home alone with my parents and often remember months of them not speaking to each other. When all five of us were in the house, it was OK, but when it was just the three of us, I felt an immense responsibility to keep my mother happy while, at the same time, please my father in the hope that he would say kind words, praise me, and tell me that he loved me. He never did. My interpretation of that was that I can't have been doing enough; I wasn't good enough and needed to try harder and do more. Not once as a child did I ever think that this may have been because he was incapable of showing love. Not once did I think that actually, it wasn't that he wasn't praising me because I wasn't good enough, but because he just didn't know how from his own childhood. It's only in adulthood, having survived a narcissistic marriage, that I've realized I've been living with a wounded inner child and that my childhood had such a significant impact on my adult relationships.

The concept of the inner child has gained recognition as a powerful framework for understanding how our early experiences shape our adult lives. This inner child represents the emotional and psychological residue of our formative years, holding the memories, beliefs, and emotional wounds from our childhood. The inner child is the embodiment of our past selves, still alive within us, influencing our thoughts, feelings, and behaviors. Do you ever feel like stamping your foot or just crying in a corner? This is often your inner child speaking and not you as the adult.

I used to cry a lot when I was with my ex-husband as I felt so alone. I used to say harsh and critical words to myself about crying like a baby when in fact this was my inner child desperately seeking out love from my husband because it took me back to not feeling love from my father. There was one incident when I was so poorly and just wanted to go to bed and be cared for. My ex-husband used to work away from home for days at a time and I knew I would struggle to look after our children. For me to even ask for help was a big deal because that took me back to my inner child wound of not feeling good enough, so I had to be on my death bed to ask. I remember having about an hour-long conversation with him because he didn't immediately respond with, 'Of course, darling, I can see how ill you are.' What he did instead was show zero emotion, even to the point that I remember crying on the living room floor and he was just looking at me like he was watching paint dry. I had the familiar feeling of 'I don't matter' – my inner child was screaming for love and safety. This crying was a way for my inner child to externalize the feelings of being unloved in the hope that someone would see and would soothe my wounds.

Traumatic Events

So many of us have an adult body with a wounded inner child – our programming – running the show. Listed below are a whole host of potential events that a child can experience and start to think are happening because of them. As we experience these, it's like putting pebbles, rocks, and boulders into an invisible backpack that no else sees, but it weighs us down and life feels heavy.

When we talk about trauma, it's not just the usual things we would think about.

Obvious causes of trauma include:

- war, natural disasters

- death of loved ones

- severe childhood emotional, physical, or sexual abuse

- neglect, betrayal, or abandonment

- parents' divorce

- experiencing or witnessing violence

- sexual assault or rape

- armed robbery

- catastrophic injuries and illness

- immobilization, casting, splinting

- prenatal stress/rejection

- birth stress, for both mother and infant

- illness of a parent, sibling, grandparent

Less obvious causes of trauma include:

- minor car accidents, falls, minor injuries

- medical or dental procedures, especially involving anesthesia, or intimate examinations

- being left alone, waiting to be fetched from school

- being lost in a strange place

- feeling unloved, criticized, unsupported, unrecognized

- parent who drinks, rages, withdraws, gambles, or who is sick, anxious, or depressed

- parent who often arrives late or breaks promises

- financial difficulties in the family

- moving house or changing schools

- birth of a sibling

- having a sibling who is more intelligent, gifted, beautiful, popular, loved

- illness, high fever, food poisoning

- death of pets

- not being picked for the team

- not being invited to a party or being teased or bullied by peers

- unfair or harsh punishment

- hurtful comments by a teacher or parent

- being rejected by a friend, boyfriend, or girlfriend[1]

How many of these events can you relate to? How heavy is your invisible backpack that you have been carrying around for years?

When we explore our attachment style, as we did in the last chapter, we also start to unpick how we interpret these events and how they impact how we feel. An early insecure attachment style can increase the negative interpretation of an event. For instance, if a child has an unemotional parent and the child develops an anxious attachment style, and then the parents get divorced, the child's attachment style also then dictates how their nervous system will react. If a child has anxious attachment, they already need more reassurance and have a dysregulated nervous system as a baseline. Factor in the divorce and these early experiences become traumatic because the child will struggle to cope even more. This has been seen in veterans who have gone to war. If they have early attachment disorders and then trauma, this impacts the prevalence of PTSD upon return.

As we can see, attachment is at the foundation of everything. It explains our programming, so we can start to navigate why we feel the way we do. It's time to go within and start to heal the unseen wounds that the narcissist in your life is shining a spotlight on.

Understanding Your Inner Wounds

In the work that I do, I look at narcissism through a trauma-informed and Internal Family Systems (IFS) lens. IFS transformed how I saw all humans and it changed my life in so many ways. IFS is an integrative, evidence-based part of psychotherapy developed by Dr. Richard Schwartz in the 1980s.[2] It allowed me to see my own perceived flaws more kindly and understand narcissists in a different way. IFS suggests that we all have 'parts' or sub-personalities, led by a core self. We may know this as the true self, the authentic self, the source, or the essence of who we are. Self isn't something that is created – it is innate in all of us. Just like if we have a cloudy day, it doesn't mean the sun isn't behind the clouds, your self – your sunshine – is always there, but sometimes it's not visible.

Ideally, we should all be navigating through life as our true and present self, feeling safe even though there are challenges along the way. Our true self has eight wonderful traits that we are born with – they are always there and are not taught:

1. Confidence

2. Compassion

3. Clarity

4. Creativity

5. Curiosity

6. Confidence

7. Clarity

8. Courage

If we're not living as our true self, if it feels unsafe to simply be ourselves, it's because wounded younger parts of us that have interpreted and perceived behavior from our parents, caregivers, friends, teachers, or family in a certain way hold on to the burden of painful memories that have been interpreted from the past. These core emotional wounds then stay stuck – or frozen – in your inner system at a particular age, even though you continue to grow and get older.

To heal with IFS, we need to understand when that wounding happened and how we can change the interpreted experience of the core self at the time it became wounded and fragmented. When did you last feel totally safe to just simply be you? So many times, clients have said to me, 'Never,' and sometimes it's as far back as when they were three years old.

We call these core emotional wounds 'exiles.' Common exiles are:

- 'I'm not good enough.'

- 'I'm unlovable.'

- 'I'm worthless.'

- 'I'm not important.'

You may have slightly different interpretations and that's OK – whatever feels relevant for you. These exiles are what our inner system never wants to feel and so the protector 'parts' within our system will then start to take over to minimize our core wound and soothe any emotional pain we may be in. In IFS there are two types of protector parts, which I like to refer to as our 'protector response': the managers and the firefighters.

Managers show up daily for us and work consistently hard to navigate and stop the exile being triggered and us feeling that pain. They act to keep us secure and minimize, soothe, and diminish the potential of feeling the pain of the exile. They work hard to control people, situations, and events, and carry a huge burden of responsibility to keep us in the least amount of pain possible. Their motto is 'never again.' These protectors are proactive and responses include:

- perfectionism

- people-pleasing

- high-achieving

- self-sabotage

- inner critic

- planner

- judgmental

- caretaker

- anxiety

- depression

- social media addict

Firefighters spring into action when the core wound, the exile, has been triggered, the nervous system is overwhelmed with emotions, and the managers are unable to stop the pain of the exile. Firefighters are usually destructive and aim to put out the 'fire' on the pain. Their motto is 'when all else fails.' These protectors are reactive and responses include:

- pain

- dissociation

- emotional eating

- addiction

- drugs or alcohol

- overexercise

- anger

- self-harm

- sex

- obsessive compulsive disorder (OCD)

- overspending

This is how we all are as human beings – we all have a self, we have exile, core inner child wounds, and then our protector response to try to soothe and minimize that pain.

My exile was me not feeling good enough as a child and this became the all-encompassing deep pain that my nervous system didn't want me to feel. Enter my protector response to try to soothe and minimize that pain. My protector responses as a child were people-pleasing, high-achieving, and perfectionism. Surely, I thought, if I pleased my father, behaved perfectly, and achieved high grades, then he would say how proud he was of me? He didn't because he wasn't capable of doing so. I didn't know that as a child, so these responses became active and heightened as they strived to get my father to praise me and, in turn, soothe my core emotional exile wound of not feeling good enough.

As I grew older, other responses appeared as other people in my life triggered my not-good-enough wound – these have included emotional eating, anger, self-harm, and dissociation, to name a few. In fact, I think I lived decades totally disconnected from my body in a state of emotional numbness and merely functioning and existing, yet no one would have known as I would always be smiling.

I used to feel such shame around my protector reponses as I thought I could control them. I didn't realize they were there to protect me from feeling my inner child wound, which the narcissist highlighted and became my version of danger. Learning that I had no 'bad parts' was such a revelation to me. Actually, what I did have was a system that had been working hard for decades to minimize any of my emotional exile pains.

My protector responses like people-pleasing, perfectionism, and high-achieving were magnets to the narcissist as I would be the best girlfriend ever – if I pleased everyone and was perfect, then surely no one, including the narcissist, would trigger my core inner child wound of not feeling good enough. But, of course, this was often not enough, and so other more destructive protector responses would take over, like self-harm.

It was life-changing for me to realize that I was not an angry person, that I was not a self-harmer, that I was not an emotional eater – that, actually, these were all parts of me trying to protect myself from a core emotional pain that my inner system thought would be too painful to feel. It massively helped lift the shame as I started to understand that, even though I was an adult now, my inner child was still ruling the roost based on my interpretation of past experiences.

My exile inner child wound and subsequent protector responses meant that I was completely abandoning myself. It wasn't safe to be me because, as me, I didn't receive love from my father – I had to do extra, I had to do more. This self-abandonment became my driving force to seek out external validation from others because I didn't know that simply being me, Caroline, was good enough. When we people-please, we're looking for that external validation because we've learned that we're not good enough simply for being who we are. Most people pleasers have anxious attachment style and there's a definite correlation between anxious attachment and being a magnet to a narcissist as we seek the external approval and validation from the narcissist, who love bombs us with that at the start (see *page 13*). This is known as codependency – an umbrella term we can give to someone who has a lot of reactive protector responses, such as people-pleasing, perfectionism, and guilt, and who abandons themselves and seeks out others to make them feel safe and good enough.

No one is born a codependent; we are a collection of these types of behaviors triggered by early traumatic experiences. The table opposite shows a list of potential traits or responses that an individual may have when they have interpreted that they are not good enough. Can you relate to any?

IFS was a piece of my healing that was truly transformational and it's why I'm so passionate about it. IFS is non-shaming and non-pathologizing (for example, I wasn't diagnosed with borderline personality disorder, which a lot of people are when they're in narcissistic relationships). Instead, IFS allows for the realization that we're always behaving in a protective way from our past experiences. There's nothing bad about any of us, even the narcissist, as we'll come to see; it's just our inner system always working for us to protect, minimize, and diminish internal emotional pain. IFS allows for curiosity around why those protective responses are there in the first place; maybe they were needed at three years old or nine years old, but we can ask ourselves are they really needed now?

IFS gave me a greater understanding of the inner workings of my psyche and helped me to understand that I had a core self – the

A Breakdown of Codependent Traits That Are Adaptive Protective Responses		
People-pleasing	Planner	Stubborn
Approval-seeking	Self-harm	Suspicious
Peacemaker	Addiction	Distrusting
Caretaking	Procrastinator	Questioning
Manipulative	Anger	OCD
Projection	Insecure	Defensive
Controlling	Shame	Self-hate
Lack of boundaries	Impulsive	Hypersensitive
Dismissive	Childlike	Paranoid
Jealousy	Imposter syndrome	Guilt
Perfectionist	Disconnected	Remorse
Inner critic	Alone	Highly judgmental
Emotional eater	Depression	Lack of insight
Overspending	Pain	Over-responsibility
Victim	Competitive	Promiscuous
Social media scrolling	Passive-aggressive	
High-achiever	Argumentative	

truest form of me, my source – that had, at some point, interpreted that it wasn't safe to show up as that. As humans, we're built for survival and to move away from pain towards pleasure; enter our protective responses to try to do just that, whether it's for a second or for years. These protective responses are what are collectively given the diagnosis of 'narcissist,' or 'codependent,' or 'borderline personality disorder,' or 'bipolar,' and so on.

IFS transformed how I saw myself. Rather than thinking I was a broken woman, I came to see that I was a woman who had pain and that my body was doing the best it could to minimize that pain. Just like I did, my wish for you is to use IFS in your life (and with your children if you have them) to understand that there are no bad parts of you – they're all there for a reason.

Narcissist Behaviors

Narcissists are also individuals who have experienced some kind of trauma, which then creates an exile and their inner system also goes into full-blown protection mode. The difference is that, for these individuals, their protector responses become very abusive and, as we explored in Chapter 1, shows up as things like coercive control, gaslighting, manipulation, and adultery. The table opposite shows some examples of the traits or protector responses of a narcissist. These are behaviors that show up for an individual to distract from and soothe their pain. Remember, in my view, narcissism is not a diagnosis, but a group of abusive protector responses that we can collectively call 'narcissistic.'

You'll see that there are some crossovers with codependents because a narcissist is an individual who has also completely abandoned themselves, but their brains are wired differently to that of codependents.

Brain scans have shown that the brains of narcissists have fewer mirror neurons and a complete lack of empathy, although they can fake cognitive empathy to get what they need. Mirror neurons are like little mirrors inside your brain. When you watch someone do something, like smile or wave, your mirror neurons help you understand and feel what that person is doing or feeling. It's like your brain copies their actions and emotions, so you can better understand them. Mirror neurons help us connect with others because they let us 'mirror' or imitate what we see and understand how others are feeling. They help us share emotions and actions with the people around us, almost like having a secret language in our brains that helps us understand each other better. Unlike narcissists, codependents tend to be empaths and have an increased amount of mirror neurons in the brain.

A Breakdown of Narcissistic Traits		
Lack of empathy	Pessimist	Vindictive
Lying	Optimist	Competitive
Manipulative	Sarcastic	Entitled
Projection	Addiction	Grandiose
Contempt	Rage	Passive-aggressive
Controlling	Anger	Condescending
Gaslighting	Insecure	Self-centered
Lack of boundaries	Shame	Argumentative
Dismissive	Impulsive	Lack of self
Jealousy	Childlike	Hypersensitive
Coercive control	Imposter syndrome	Paranoid
Careless	Disconnected	No guilt
Envious	Alone	No remorse
Generous	Cheating	Highly judgmental
Cheap	Arrogant	Lack of insight
Victim	Exploitative	No responsibility
Superficial	Lack of responsibility	Stubborn

There's one other key difference between codependents and narcissists, and that is ownership and responsibility. The narcissist will think that their protective responses are not protective as they have no wounds. They feel they're only behaving like this because of you – that if you conformed to them, they wouldn't need to show up like this. In theory, what they are saying is that it's your fault. A codependent, on the other hand, will be able to understand the IFS concept, recognize their core wounds from childhood, be open to that work, and have a sense of ownership and responsibility.

I know that I was far from perfect in my relationship with my ex-husband, but I also know that I can take ownership of that and understand now why I was behaving in that way – because of my childhood trauma and attachment style. Ownership meant that I could do the work and come from a place now where my nervous system is far more regulated, and I know that the narcissist's behavior was never a reflection of me at all; I had just interpreted it as that.

There's no excuse for narcissistic abuse at all – abuse is abuse is abuse – but when you can understand that the narcissist is also a deeply wounded individual, you can start to see that their behavior is never a reflection of you. It's not your fault. You are just the tool for them to use to project their pain onto, so you can behave in a way to minimize their pain. But this is not a life you now want to live. You want to heal, thrive, and flourish – and this is all possible when you follow all the interventions and exercises in this book.

Why Narcissists Are Drawn to Codependents

Codependents have a strong desire to please others, which can make us vulnerable to the manipulation and control of a narcissist – the cycle of abuse we discussed in Chapter 1. Codependents want to give, give, give in the hope that the recipient then behaves in a certain way, soothing their wounds, and their interpretation can be that they are then good enough. This is like a magnet to a narcissist because narcissists want to take, take, take. It's a match made in heaven as each one taking and giving soothes each other's wounds with that action.

The love bombing and the hoovering that we explored in Chapter 1 all soothe the codependent's wounds while the narcissist hooks you in. The narcissist will groom you so you become addicted to their charm and grand gestures, feeding the hole in your soul. The narcissist knows exactly how to ensnare a codependent who is coming from a place of deep inner childhood wounds, of not feeling good enough.

The codependent's constant striving for external validation can be emotionally exhausting and lead to feelings of anxiety and depression. You may become so enmeshed in the narcissist's web of control that you lose sight of what a healthy relationship looks like.

Recovery from codependency and from seeking validation from others can be a difficult and painful process, but it is possible. You're in the right place to finally start to lift that shame, and heal and thrive after narcissistic abuse.

TRAUMA BONDING

The cycle of hormone release in the narcissistic abuse cycle (see *page 12*) becomes a physiological addiction to the hormones. This is what we call a trauma bond and what makes it so difficult to separate from a narcissist, whether that be a parent or romantic partner.

Trauma bonding is a powerful force that keeps you trapped and addicted to being in a relationship with a narcissist. The hypothalamus in the brain secretes a chemical peptide while going through narcissistic abuse, which the body then craves and keeps us trauma-bonded to the abuser.

This type of toxic bond occurs when the abuser alternates between creating highs and lows within the relationship and offers reward or punishment as they deem fit – as we saw in the abuse cycle. I experienced this many times with my husband and it can make you feel like you're going crazy.

The narcissist will train you that happiness is solely dependent on how well they can service and please you. The bond can long outlive the relationship, leaving you craving comfort from the very person who hurt you.

We actually become physiologically addicted to narcissists – addicted to the struggle and not feeling good enough in relationships. This comes again from childhood wiring and is not your fault. If you stay with an abuser, you're not weak. This is your nervous system feeling like it's safer to stay than leave and, sometimes, in that moment, it is. But you deserve to be treated with love and respect. The tools in this book will help you break the trauma bond that keeps you trapped in a toxic relationship. If you're feeling overwhelmed in this moment, please reach out for help (see *Resources, page 239*).

A Narcissist Does Not Change

A question I get asked A LOT is 'Will the narcissist ever change?' The quick answer is no – there's nothing you can do to change a narcissist. This may seem sad and lacking compassion, but it really isn't. It's not that, as a therapist and coach, I wouldn't love to help a person heal their exile part, but I have never seen anyone who is a narcissist be completely cured. For someone to heal or change, they need to acknowledge that they need to change, and this means not just pretending to do so as a means of hoovering you back into the cycle of narcissistic abuse.

As we've explored, and as I'm sure you will have experienced, narcissists take zero ownership or responsibility for their actions – they have deep wounds that they can't feel so they project all their pain onto others instead of owning it.

This is why I look at narcissistic abuse a little differently, in a way which honors our compassionate, human side but doesn't give us false hope that they will change. I know this may be so hard to hear because, as a codependent, you want to believe that they could change, but sadly no clinical research suggests they can.

There have been cases of narcissists having medication to help, but they're still unable to have a healthy relationship. If someone ever tells you that a narcissist will change, this is gaslighting because it's simply not true or they were never a narcissist in the first place.

> *A narcissist will never change, but the*
> *power to heal is within YOU.*

So, if you know you're dealing with a narcissist, focus your energy on YOU and what YOU can control, not on the narcissist, whom you can't.

HOW TO LEAVE A TOXIC RELATIONSHIP

Leaving a toxic relationship is not as easy as literally making the decision, packing, and leaving; instead, it's a process. There are many parameters to consider because, if toxicity or abuse is involved, safety has to be the number one priority.

Planning is absolutely essential

Photocopy bank statements, passports, birth certificates, and so on, and store the paperwork somewhere safe where your partner will not find it, like the boot of your car, or ask a supportive friend or family member to store it at their house. Make sure you have your finances in place and either an alternative place to live or somewhere you can move out to safely, such as a refuge or with friends or family.

Seek support and help

Ending a relationship can feel massively triggering with feelings of shame and judgment of both oneself and of what others may say about your failed relationship, especially if children are involved. It doesn't help that, as a society, terms such as 'broken home' are used. Homes are not broken if there is toxicity, and society should support, not judge. Surround yourself with friends and family who understand, not those who to want gossip or dissect everything.

Think about timing

Choose a time that is safest for you to let them know the relationship is over. That may mean you choose to move out when they're at work, or you may have a friend or family member with you as you tell them.

Go no contact or extreme modified contact

The only way to truly detach from the dark reality of the narcissist is to cut off all contact with them. This means shutting all the doors on them – social media, email, phone, text messaging, and any other avenue you may have. You have to be steadfast in this and try not to cave in. Give an inch and they will take 10 miles. You must control the situation. No matter how much the narcissist may try to love bomb and hoover you back into the relationship, stay strong and recognize that you deserve more. If you have children, extreme modified contact is advised. Treat your relationship with your ex like a business partnership. Monitor your phone calls with a filter, direct any correspondence to a new email address created solely for the ex-partner, and only check in at set times a week. Direct everything else through your legal team if necessary.

Allow yourself to grieve

Once you've left the relationship, it will feel strange and sad, so allow yourself to grieve the loss of the relationship. Grief is all part of the process. Often it's not necessarily the toxic person you're missing, but the hopes and dreams that you'd created by being in that relationship. It will feel hard, especially if trauma bonding is present (see *page 57*), as people literally get addicted to struggle and toxicity, and not being in that toxic relationship can feel alien to your body. You can reach out to a professional to support you through your feelings.

Remember: The narcissist is not your trauma. You've been abused by an individual with abusive protector responses, that we can then collectively call narcissism, but they will never change these responses. Our personal power lies in understanding why we react the way we do and how these destructive protector responses come up for us. How amazing is your inner system that's been trying to protect you for many years, decades even? While this may have made you a magnet to a narcissist, you can now start to unpack this, lift the shame and self-blame, and stop abandoning yourself.

After recognizing your attachment style, this is your next step in healing from narcissistic abuse. It's my hope that this chapter has shown you that you can still keep leaning into the beautiful soul that I know you are and find some solace in the knowledge that the narcissist in your life is a narcissist because of their childhood and this was nothing to do with you not being good enough. There are no bad parts of you, only protector responses working hard to protect you from feeling a deep, emotional pain.

In the next chapter, we'll deepen our relationship with these protective responses by doing some work at a nervous system level.

CHAPTER 4

Understanding the Nervous System

Now you understand that narcissism is the naming of a collection of protector responses that are abusive, and that the narcissist won't change, we can focus on why it feels so hard to heal from narcissistic abuse. In this chapter, we'll explore the nervous system and why we feel the way we do. Our nervous system is at the core of our narcissistic abuse experience.

In school, we're taught so much about the human body, but we never learn about the nervous system. If we did, I feel it would enable us to lift so much of the pain, judgment, and shame that so many of us end up carrying, thinking that we're weak and a failure – because we're not. In this chapter, I hope to show you what an awesome human being you are and why we all have an innate capacity to heal when we give understanding and space for that to happen.

What Is the Nervous System?

Our nervous system, a complex network of nerves and cells, serves as the body's communication system. It regulates and responds to various stimuli, including stressors and threats. Our nervous system is also at the heart of our lived experiences and tells the story of our past. If we're not living our life as our true and present self, as we explored in the last chapter, we know that our past has not been processed and so we keep on reacting in the present as if it's still happening now. The body is constantly reliving and reacting as opposed to remembering and regulating.

As human beings, we're wired for survival so, when we don't feel safe or we perceive threats and danger, our nervous system takes over and goes into protect mode. It will override any logic in any given moment. This is why you can't 'think' your way out of healing trauma. It's a somatic (bodily) experience. It's why, even though cognitively we may look back and know that things are not our fault, it doesn't mean our body now knows this, too. This is why, when we work with trauma like narcissistic abuse, we have to work with the body and the nervous system.

The nervous system response is completely involuntary and you can't stop it, because when your past has not been processed and integrated, it dictates your actions. Many of us feel so much shame when we feel like this, but actually it's just your body trying to protect you. Your body is always working for you, just like your protector response.

What is it about a narcissist's behavior that makes our nervous system feel it needs to react in a certain way? To answer this, we need to understand how our nervous system works and how we can shift nervous system states so we can heal after narcissistic abuse.

How the narcissist damages your nervous system

Remember, there are no bad parts of us, only adaptive responses to minimize and reduce the deep emotional pain we may be feeling and carrying. This is true for you and also for a narcissist. Our autonomic nervous system (which controls unconscious processes, such as breathing and blood pressure) is basically telling the story of our past experiences in our visible reactions of fight, flight, or freeze and even fawn.

When we go into a trauma response, it means our inner system is detecting and perceiving danger. Now, if we were being attacked, this is good and we want this to happen. The problem when we are with a narcissist, however, is that we're often not in actual life-threatening danger, but our nervous system responds as if we are, like a wild animal would. The narcissist brings us a felt sense in our body that the situation is dangerous and triggers a past emotional wound. If there's no actual danger and we're reacting, we're no longer in the present moment, but back in the past, and our nervous system then responds in what it feels is the most appropriate way.

Think about a time when you have seen the narcissist and your heart starts to race and you get pins and needles in your fingers and toes. This is an example of a somatic trauma response. You're not in actual danger, but your nervous system is sensing that there's a potential for pain, so it's alerting your body to get ready to look out for you.

NOSE BREATHING

This simple breathwork technique encourages mindfulness and relaxation without the need for counting. It's an excellent way to connect with your breath, reduce stress, and promote a sense of inner peace in the moment.

- Find a quiet and comfortable place to sit or lie down. Close your eyes gently if you like. Keep your mouth closed throughout the practice. Breathe in and out exclusively through your nose.

- Begin by taking a few normal breaths through your nose. Let the breath flow naturally without trying to control it. Focus on the sensation of the air entering and leaving your nostrils. Feel the coolness as you inhale and the warmth as you exhale.

- Gradually start to deepen your breath. Make your breaths a bit deeper and more deliberate, but still comfortable. Inhale through your nose, allowing your abdomen to rise, and exhale through your nose, letting go of any tension. You may want to place a hand on your abdomen for this.

- Relax and repeat. Continue with this pattern of deep inhales and relaxed exhales through your nose. There's no need to force or rush it; just let your breath flow naturally.

- Stay present. If your mind starts to wander, gently bring your focus back to the sensation of your breath. Each inhale brings in fresh energy, and each exhale releases stress and tension.

Practice this exercise regularly. Dedicate a few minutes each day to this nose-breathing technique. As you practice regularly, you'll notice an increased sense of calm and centeredness in your daily life.

Our nervous system works on a hierarchy – what I call the 'Traffic Lights of Tolerance™.' The Traffic Lights of Tolerance™ represent the three main parts of our autonomic nervous system:

1. Feeling safe and connected in the green light

2. Fight-or-flight in the yellow light

3. Freeze in the red light

This is based on Dr. Stephen Porges's Polyvagal Theory.[1] The green light is our social engagement system, when we feel safe and connected to others. It's a branch of our ventral vagus nerve, which runs down the back of our neck and innervates our face and above our diaphragm. This is when we feel present and safe, and we're living our life as our true and present self. Think 'green for grounded.'

But the moment a part of our brain called the limbic system (our emotional brain, which contains our amygdala and hippocampus) feels threat or potential danger, we shift into the yellow light – our fight-or-flight response in our sympathetic nervous system. This is when we start to pump out hormones like cortisol and adrenalin to get ready to fight or run away. We need the cortisol so we're ready to protect ourselves as we mobilize that energy. The moment we shift into the yellow light, we move from the present into the past. Whatever's happening in that moment we perceive as reminding us of an old emotional wound, an exile inner child, and our body needs to protect us.

With narcissistic abuse, we can move into fight-or-flight even if we're not in any actual physical danger from the narcissist. Instead, the narcissist is triggering a past core exile wound causing our nervous system to relive it and react. Our body fills with cortisol and we start to feel like our heart is racing faster as energy starts to go to the limbs in anticipation of needing to fight or flee. If we stay in this response long term, as many of us do, it can lead to chronic illness and disease as it causes inflammation in the body. Over 80 per cent of disease and illness is caused by us remaining in these stress responses even though there is no actual danger, which is why I see so many people who have experienced narcissistic abuse with some form of chronic illness.[2]

If we continue to perceive threat and danger, we shift into the red light – a freeze response. This is another branch of the vagus nerve, called the dorsal vagal. At this point, it becomes about purely protecting our major organs and we can start to feel like we have no energy. We're in survival mode here even though, for most of us, there is still no actual danger – it's the perceived danger and reminder of our past emotional wounds. We start to become smaller and isolate ourselves, just like a wild animal may want to hide and stay safe from a predator. In a freeze response, even getting out of bed in the morning can feel like you're about to climb Mount Everest. You're not failing or weak at this stage. All of these responses are adaptive responses to your interpretation of the present moment as threatening or dangerous.

Most people who are still experiencing narcissistic abuse, or who have just realized they are, are often in a freeze response – in the red light – because they've often spent years living in survival mode. This coping mechanism allows you to avoid triggering the abuser and protects you from further harm. But it can also prevent your healing process and moving on from the trauma. It's therefore important to recognize this and use the tools and strategies in this book to help break free from it.

As an example of the traffic light response, if an antelope was out in the wild and a lion started to chase it, it would initially shift into a flight response to try to run away to safety. If it was caught, it would enter a fight response to try to keep it safe. Then, if the antelope was still not safe, it would shift into its red light – the antelope would freeze and play dead, again still trying to stay alive. The hope would be that the lion would think that it had killed its prey and would relax after the chase, giving the antelope the opportunity to shift from red back into yellow, the flight response, and run away. Usually the antelope would then shake off and discharge any sympathetic energy and go back to feeling safe and its own business.

If only this was the case for us humans! However, because we have a ventral vagal part of our nervous system and a front part of our brain called the neocortex, we overthink and stop and suppress this natural movement through the hierarchy of the nervous system. How you then behave is your nervous system trying to keep you safe, so if you numb out – retreat, drink, eat, rage, and so on – these are all responses to your threat of danger and protector responses showing up to keep you as safe as possible.

Nervous system dysregulation

In the modern world, our nervous systems are often bombarded with a continuous stream of information and stressors, pushing us into a state of constant fight, flight, or freeze – from the narcissist to social media, the news, and even our children and family members. This perpetual state of hyper- or hypo-arousal – known as dysregulation – can lead to a host of physical and mental health issues.

To understand the importance of reclaiming yourself at a nervous system level, we must first acknowledge the consequences of living in a state of chronic stress from narcissistic abuse and, likely, even further back from then. The nervous system is highly affected when you're in a long-term relationship with a narcissist, and you may experience a range of emotional and physical symptoms:

- The constant emotional abuse and manipulation by the narcissist can lead to the development of chronic stress, anxiety, and depression.

- Long-term exposure to a narcissist's behavior can cause the brain's amygdala to become overactive, leading to hypervigilance and increased fear responses.

- The constant state of alertness and hypervigilance may also lead to sleep disturbances and difficulty relaxing.

- Prolonged stress can lead to elevated levels of cortisol, which, in turn, can lead to inflammation and chronic illnesses like heart disease, fibromyalgia, and irritable bowel syndrome (IBS).

- In extreme cases, long-term exposure to a narcissist's behavior can lead to C-PTSD and long-lasting effects on the nervous system's functioning.

Our body is an *amazing* machine and wants to heal, but when it's dealing with past trauma, things can go a bit haywire. Chronic stress can affect the functioning of the autonomic nervous system, which controls involuntary bodily functions like breathing, heart rate, and digestion. An imbalanced autonomic nervous system can result in digestive issues, sleep disturbances, and cardiovascular problems. This is why I believe I had a diagnosis of IBS, non-alcoholic fatty liver disease, and long QT syndrome, which is a heart condition. I'm convinced all of these were stress- and trauma-related.

According to renowned addiction expert, speaker, and author Dr. Gabor Maté, 80 per cent of autoimmune disorders are diagnosed in female people pleasers.[3] This is a huge statistic and shows that, if we have a strong people-pleasing part of us, it can lead to us suppressing our voice and internalizing that pain. Eventually, that voice will start to scream in the form of a chronic illness like an autoimmune disorder. I was a chronic people pleaser and internalized my voice as I needed others to like me and deemed my only sense of worth was in how others saw me. I have now reversed my non-alcoholic fatty liver disease and IBS and am working on my heart condition. While I've been told I have this condition for life, I don't accept this – I truly believe we have tremendous healing powers within our body when we know how to tap into them. This is what I teach and work with my clients on. Healing from narcissistic abuse is a journey, and managing chronic illness is just one part of that journey.

You are strong and resilient, and you deserve to live a life free from abuse and chronic illness.

Our Nervous System as a Baby

When we're born and come into this world, our red and yellow lights of fight, flight, and freeze are already raring to go within our nervous system in anticipation of protecting us and keeping us safe. However, as mammals, we can't do anything for ourselves when we're born, so we're totally reliant on our parents and caregivers. This means the green light, the ventral vagal part of our nervous system, has to be taught to us by our parents and caregivers. They need to nurture us, love us, and speak kindly and softly to us so we can start to feel that the world is safe. Our parents need to show us that their love is unconditional so that we can learn to co-regulate with them to feel safe enough to self-regulate as we go through our development as a child.

The problem is that sometimes our parents are also carrying their own trauma and have never themselves been taught how to feel and show love. So, as an adult, if you had parents who were not emotionally mature enough to show you the love, safety, and security you needed to help make you feel safe, why would you ever feel totally safe?

This works on a spectrum. You could have one caregiver who was nurturing, but another who was emotionally unavailable. This was my experience and, as an adult, it had far-reaching consequences. My not-feeling-good-enough wound was so painful to feel as a child that anyone trying to make me feel like that as an adult meant that I would react in a trauma response, just as if I was being attacked.

It's important to note that this isn't about shaming or demonizing your parents or caregivers – or laying the blame at anyone's door. Instead, it's about truly looking at what could have been your perception of your parental behavior and whether they helped tone that ventral vagal part of your nervous system, the green light, so that you would feel safe and loved simply for being you. If our parents didn't teach us to feel safe and connected, we constantly live our lives in a perpetual state of fight/flight or freeze until we do our own work to tone our ventral vagus nerve so we can start to feel safe again. This is why many of us feel so much shame when we're experiencing narcissistic abuse because we get angry one minute, cry the next, or don't want to get out of bed, or see or speak to anyone. I know this, because this was once me.

THE IMPACT OF NARCISSISTIC ABUSE ON CHILDREN

I know many of you have children and this is such an important point to make here. When your children are with the narcissist, it can look externally like they are really well-behaved. Then, when your children come back to you, they can often start to play up; they may present as more anxious or angry, and you can start to doubt and question yourself as an adult.

But think about the hierarchy of the nervous system: Your children are actually in a freeze response with the narcissist, protecting their little nervous systems from feeling pain, and this almost looks like a faux ventral vagal state but it's NOT. It's freeze – and unless you're trained to know or recognize this, the narcissist can make out the children are worse behaved with you. I've seen this scenario many times in court with the narcissist saying, 'But they're always fine with me.' If professionals don't understand abuse and are not trauma-informed, it can look like the children are fine with the narcissist.

In truth, the children *are* 'worse' behaved with you, but that's because they feel safer as they move from the red light with the narcissist to the yellow light and the sympathetic response when they're with you. This comes out as more overt behavior and can actually seem harder, but take comfort in knowing that this is because you're the safe parent. While this book is written for you, my hope is that you'll use it to heal yourself and help heal the next generation with your new understanding and tools to do so.

The protector responses that we met in the last chapter only show up when we shift into a trauma response because our system then perceives that it's unsafe for us to stay living as our true self. We shift into the yellow or red and a protector response will show up. The problem comes when the protector response remains stuck in our system, protecting a wounded younger part of us in conjunction with a trauma response. Examples of human behavior in a trauma response include:

- Fight: anger, anxiety

- Flight: running away, slamming doors

- Freeze: dissociation, depression

These protector responses are actually stopping us from completing the trauma response cycle. For example, if we were neglected or felt unloved, that would have felt dangerous to us as a child. But it wouldn't have been safe in that moment to tell our parents to 'F$%* off'! That would have brought even more potential danger, so a dissociation part may have come in to protect you, which, as we've seen, then remains stuck in your nervous system.

Mapping out our protector response against our nervous system can really help us understand our own inner system, why we react and feel the way we do, and that we're actually responding to what we've learned and perceived from our childhood. I call this SELF Navigation Mapping™. It's a true gift to yourself to start to understand your nervous system and how protector responses show up for you so that you can look at yourself with a renewed admiration and a deeper kindness. This is your next brave step in the healing process.

SELF Navigation Mapping™

SELF Navigation Mapping™ is a process that I created to help us look at our nervous system states and how our protector response fits within that model. For instance, a depression protector response would sit in the red light (the freeze response) because we have no energy when we're depressed, and an anxiety part would sit in the yellow light (in a fight/flight response in the sympathetic part of our nervous system) as our body is flooded with cortisol when we're anxious, ready to fight or flee.

SELF Navigation Mapping™ enables us to look at ourselves with no shame and more compassion. We start to understand this isn't as simple as the present situation with a narcissist and just 'getting on with it.' It brings into account our childhood and how we may have created inner child wounds — exiles — and that, as humans, we are driven to survive and move away from pain, especially emotional and relational pain. It considers the complex layers of attachment from our childhood and our perception of parental or caregiver behavior, which in turn can create exiles, such as those explored in the previous chapter (*see page 48*).

SELF Navigation Mapping™ helps you understand your system so you can start to lift the shame and stop abandoning yourself. It allows you to have a bird's eye view of which nervous system states are more dominant for you and which protector responses keep showing up with the most loving of intentions to minimize your emotional pain, but which are often destructive behaviors.

We used to think that, once we had a belief, it was wired in for life. In fact, this is how cognitive behavioral therapy (CBT) came about – cognitively looking at behavior and symptoms, and changing the symptoms with different behavior. What this did not do was work on the root cause. But we now know with neuroscience that we can change that. This is why somatic work, working in the body at a nervous system level, is so imperative and exactly how I help people heal and thrive after narcissistic abuse.

Mapping your system

Take a look back at the four core emotional wounds on page 48. Is there one in particular that you can relate to? It could be more than one or even all four. This is your starting point: You know what your core emotional wound and belief about yourself is, and you know that if anyone triggers that core wound, your protective responses are going to show up.

Once you feel you know what your core wound is, grab a notebook and pen or a digital device. Below are some overarching protector responses. Write down all of those that you can relate to, and please feel free to add your own if you have any others.

Guilty	Impatient	Social media addict
Organizer	Martyr	Dissociation
Stubborn	Liar	Analyzer
Procrastinator	Indecisive	Overachiever
Spending money	Overexercise	Pessimist
Perfectionism	Comparing	Isolating
Rebellious	Catastrophizer	Planner
Controlling	Bullying	Suspicious
Jealous	Doer	Imposter

Academic	Defensive	People-pleasing
Caretaker	Eating disorders	Angry
Emotional eating	Judgmental	Gossip
Training junkie	Inner critic	Self-harm
Addict	Worrier	Apologetic
Panic attack	Avoidant	Anxiety
OCD	Depression	Excessive drinking
Pain	Retreating	

Now, we want to map these protector responses against the Traffic Lights of Tolerance™ – your nervous system. On a fresh page, write down which core emotional wound you can relate to the most right at the top of the page. This is your root cause pain and what your version of danger is in your system – just like the lion chasing the antelope. This represents your inner child wound.

Next, write the Traffic Lights of Tolerance™ down one side of the page. Then, map out your protector responses next to the red and yellow lights. Don't get too technical on exactly which protector response needs to be in red or yellow, but the red light is freeze, so these behaviors will be lacking in energy, such as depression and dissociation, whereas the yellow parts are more mobilized energy protector responses, like anger and anxiety. The green light is where your true self sits. This is who you are when you feel safe and connected and living in the present moment as your true and present SELF. Green light responses include calmness, being able to deal with challenges, and being connected, grounded, and present.

I've included an example map of my own core emotional wounds overleaf for you. I created this as I was healing from narcissistic abuse.

Inner child wounds: I am not good enough; I am unlovable	
Traffic Lights of Tolerance™	Protector responses
Freeze: red light (dorsal vagal)	People-pleasing Perfectionist Dissociation Depression High-achieving
Fight/flight: yellow light (sympathetic)	Anger Anxiety Emotional eating Self-harm
Safe: green light (ventral vagal)	

Take some time on this step to really understand your core emotional wound, your protector responses, and the fact that these show up to keep you safe from your version of danger. I used to think I was weak and just couldn't cope. Creating my map meant that I could see how hard my system had been working over the years to protect my wounded inner child based on my wired-in beliefs about myself from my parents and caregivers, and that I was not weak or a failure.

This is the power of self-healing: When you keep on healing your inner child, working on a flexible nervous system, you can create so much capacity in your system that, when these things happen, when the narcissist says what a bad parent you are or they try to recruit an army of flying monkeys, you know AND feel that this not a reflection of you and is actually a projection of their pain onto you.

I hope you can now see how hard your system has been working for you and never against you, even if it's felt like that at times. I know many of you will feel shame about some of your protector responses because that's what society wants you to feel, but you are a beautiful human being with a capacity to heal.

Mapping your inner system with your nervous system and your protector reponse is an essential step when healing from narcissistic abuse as it enables you to see the inner workings of how you operate – and we can't change what we are not aware of.

Can you see how the jigsaw is coming together?

- Attachment wounds

- Protector response

- Nervous system regulation

All three areas integrate to keep you safe from your past interpretation of childhood experiences, but all of this is *learned* process, meaning we can *unlearn* and integrate this into our system for secure attachment, a regulated and flexible nervous system, and calmer protector responses.

It is possible. This is why you're here; now is your time.

The next few chapters may bring up emotions, so be kind to yourself and go slow. I know that we want to heal 'yesterday' as we're sick of feeling the way that we do, but I've seen too many clients who have gone too quickly, with the best of intentions, and this has caused their nervous system to shut down. This is exactly what trauma is: When too much happens, too fast, and the nervous system doesn't have the capacity to cope.

Please trust the process, even if it feels slower than you would like. My wish for you is to have deep and long-lasting healing, not just feel good in one moment as you feel validated; we want deep healing at a nervous system level.

In Part II we're going to start working on reparenting that wounded inner child so that you're no longer riled in the present by an unhealed exile and learn how you can start to regulate your emotions. It's important to note here that healing from abuse doesn't mean you forget; it doesn't mean you won't feel certain emotions forevermore. Instead, healing from abuse is about integrating what happened to you into your body so you can fully recognize, both in your brain *and* body, that it was NOT your fault.

It's time to step into the next part of your healing journey.

PART II

Let the Healing Begin

CHAPTER 5

Healing Your Inner Child

Breaking the cycle of attracting narcissists into your life begins with recognizing the wounds of your inner child and offering the care and nurturing you may have been lacking in the past. For you to stop behaving like the inner child, your inner child must start to feel love, safety, and security from YOU. If you're always looking to others to make you feel safe, it's risky because everyone else is dealing with their own stress and trauma. Just think about the narcissist!

Your sense of worth should come from yourself, not anyone else. That's not to say that you should become a recluse – after all, as human beings, we're wired for connection – but you shouldn't need anyone to give you your sense of worth. For this to happen, we need to go back and help that inner child know *and* feel they are lovable, good enough, worthy enough, and important enough.

In this chapter, we'll go through the steps to start to heal your inner child with love and care. We'll reparent them and give them corrective attachment experiences. We'll help our nervous system see that this was back then and that you're now an adult with different knowledge and options that may not have been accessible to you as a child. This is a powerful chapter that might bring up lots of grief and sadness because we can't actually change our childhood, so please take it at your own pace; it's deep work.

However, please know that we *can* look to change the somatic experience so that our nervous system can feel calmer and regulate more, with greater capacity and flexibility, and the protector response doesn't need to show up as much. Reparenting yourself involves giving your younger self all the things you didn't receive as a child. They can be big or small, but if they mattered to you, they matter, because you matter.

WHY INNER CHILD HEALING IS SO IMPORTANT

For many adults, the experience of repeatedly attracting narcissists into their lives can be a bewildering and emotionally painful cycle. These toxic relationships can leave you feeling drained, disempowered, and questioning your own worth. This is when protector responses will start to come in as you try to get others to show you your worth. To understand and disrupt this pattern, it's essential to explore the concept of inner child healing and the profound impact of shame, which can be a huge barrier to healing, as well as the attachment wounds that often lie at the root of these dynamics.

By creating corrective attachment experiences, you can transform your somatic experience of childhood, leading to greater emotional well-being and the ability to form healthier relationships. Our brain doesn't know if something happened last week or last year. So, by reparenting your inner child as an adult, it means you get to complete and redo that which wasn't done in your childhood. As long as your system feels that it has done so, everything shifts.

The Role of Shame: A Toxic Core Belief

Shame is a profound and often debilitating emotion closely tied to our inner child. It's a huge part of how we feel when we're abused by a narcissist because we feel weak, stupid, and a failure. One of the phrases I used to say to myself all the time when I split up from my ex-husband was: 'How could I be so stupid?' I was blaming myself and felt such deep shame that I had failed. I went to that rock-bottom place and, had it not been for my children, I wouldn't be writing this book today.

I was so critical of myself, but never realized that this was actually an inner critic part of me wanting me to stay alert and on my knees because then I had a shorter fall if anything bad happened again. If you're already at rock bottom, there really is nowhere else to go. My system thought that if I started to heal, then I may be less vigilant and something bad may happen, so this inner critic part of me was like an inner warning system. Maybe you can relate to having a harsh and critical voice too?

Over time, this voice and this place of fear and struggle became my version of safe. It had become familiar and I was addicted to struggle. I'd become physiologically addicted to the hormone release of dopamine, oxytocin, and serotonin when things were good, and cortisol and adrenalin when things were bad. This was just like the abuse cycle we explored on page 12 – breadcrumbs of pleasure, but I then needed the fix of cortisol, so I would create drama and conflict even if things started to go well to get that familiar release that was now my version of safe in my body. Our body and brain are wired for survival, and emotional safety will override anything else if our body feels unsafe.

Shame often stands as a formidable barrier to well-being and personal growth, and shows up in our deepest freeze nervous system responses. It's the belief that we are fundamentally flawed or unworthy of love and belonging. Shame frequently emerges from early experiences of rejection, humiliation, or abuse, and it can become a core aspect of our self-identity. Shame can erode your self-esteem, hinder your relationships, and even compromise your physical health. Narcissists reinforce any shame that we already have due to our past experiences.

Shame, often described as the 'master emotion,' is a pervasive and deeply uncomfortable feeling. Unlike a guilty protector part, which is focused on our actions or behavior, shame attacks our very sense of self. It feels heavy and there's even a posture to go with it called the 'posture of shame.' We hunch over, making ourselves smaller, almost so no one can see us. We look away as we don't want to be seen or look someone in the eye in case they see us for the bad person we are.

My mother had scoliosis and rheumatoid arthritis when she was alive. She had a traumatic childhood and, when I look back at her posture, though I always used to think it was because of her conditions, I'm convinced she also had this posture of shame. Even now, I have to check in with my own posture. I used to put this down to being tall, but, from all my trauma training, I know that there is a natural movement of shame and I've worked hard to eliminate it.

Take a moment now to think about your posture:

- Do you have a tendency to avoid eye contact?

- Do you consistently look down?

- Do you hunch your shoulders?

This can be a somatic sign of shame. Our muscles can move into a new state of being and this is called somatic motor amnesia. As we're constantly feeling braced with our shoulders tense, jaw clenched, shoulders rolled over, this becomes our new way of being and our muscles forget what it is like to actually feel relaxed and safe. Shame is in the red light of the Traffic Lights of Tolerance™ (*see page 67*) – in freeze – which makes sense as, if we were an animal in the wild, this is when we would want to be the smallest we could possibly be, because then the predators wouldn't see us and attack or kill us.

Shame can emerge from various sources, including childhood experiences, societal norms, or personal failures, and the narcissist will shine a great big spotlight on these.

> *When left unchecked, shame festers and takes root, negatively affecting your mental, emotional, and physical well-being.*

In narcissistic relationships, shame often plays a central role. Narcissists employ tactics that can shame you, eroding your self-esteem and reinforcing the belief that you are undeserving of love or respect. This preexisting shame can make you more susceptible to the manipulations of narcissists, creating a self-reinforcing cycle of emotional pain. Chronic stress and shame often go hand in hand, with stress further exacerbating feelings of unworthiness.

To break free from this cycle, we must first delve into inner child healing, addressing the attachment wounds and the accompanying shame that is holding us captive, before learning to regulate the nervous system through practices like mindfulness, breathing, and relaxation exercises, which we'll explore in the next chapter, and implementing the positive psychology practices outlined in Chapter 7. Combined, these will not only alleviate the weight of shame, but also set the stage for profound personal transformation and allow you to embark on a journey of self-discovery, self-compassion, and self-empowerment in Part III.

A Journey to Wholeness and Back to Self

For us to show up as secure attachment adults knowing and feeling we are good enough, we must help our inner child feel that they were worthy. If we don't do this inner child healing and reparenting, it doesn't matter how much you try to think your way out of feeling the way you do, you'll always have your inner child ruling your decisions and relationships.

Inner child healing is a process that involves recognizing and tending to those emotional wounds carried from our childhood that we started uncovering in Part I. While we can't change our past, we can transform our somatic experience of it, providing the care, nurturing, and healing that our inner child needs.

The steps below explore an array of tools and exercises for you to start to nurture and heal the emotional wounds of that inner child, validating that what you experienced has had an effect, however big or small, and that you are fully committed to this process.

Complete your trauma time line

The first step in healing your inner child is recognizing the need for healing. This may involve acknowledging the trauma and its impact on your life. It's essential to validate your emotions and experiences, understanding that healing is not only possible but necessary for your well-being. You're reading this book right now, so you're in exactly the right place for this.

This exercise asks you to look back over the years from birth at what may be contributing to your interpretation of events in a way that could have led to you attracting unhealthy relationships as an adult. Grab a journal or notepad and a pen. Think back from your birth to the present day and, in chronological order, note down anything you think may have affected you. You may not remember some as they may be preverbal, but your body will remember, so still write them down if you've heard your family tell you that this or that happened.

For instance, I was born six weeks early via caesarean section. I was heavily jaundiced and placed in an incubator. Now, I don't actually have any memories of this, but imagine a baby who is born and comes into this loud, scary world and then is placed in an incubator with very little human contact (because that's what they did back then). As a newborn baby, it was being reinforced that the world is a scary place. While I may have stopped crying, this wasn't because I had gone into the green light; it was because I'd gone into a shutdown of freeze because I was trying to stay safe.

I'm not shaming my parents and the hospital staff here – at the time, they didn't know any better. But we do now. 'Ferber-izing' your baby used to be popular: letting them cry it out. We now know that when we do this, we're reinforcing that the world is a scary place and your nervous system needs to be 'on' all the time. Again, I was brought up like this and always wondered why I was so on edge all the time. It was because it had already been wired into me that the world is unsafe so I needed to be on guard. My starting point was one of 'this world is unsafe!'

Take your time with this exercise and, if it feels too much, stop and come back to it later. I've had clients who have needed more than one piece of paper.

Once you've completed your trauma time line, take a moment to step back and look at everything you may have experienced from birth to the present day. Can you see how much your nervous system has had to contain and cope with and that you're actually incredible because you're still here, reading this book?

Take some time now to go through each event and think about how a child may have interpreted them – not through the eyes of your older and more knowledgeable self, but through the eyes of the child living with your parents and caregivers. I hope you'll start to see that we can look back at events and know that they're not our fault, but a child in certain situations may feel very differently. Acknowledge this and affirm how amazing you are because you were always good enough, lovable, worthy, and important.

This exercise is about acknowledging your past experiences and recognizing that you have been through a lot. It's no wonder, then, that you've led the life you have and ended up in a narcissistic relationship. It's only when we recognize this that we can start to be kinder to ourselves.

Visualize your inner child

Using your trauma time line, visualize your inner child at various stages of your development, from infancy to adolescence. Engage in a dialogue with your inner child, asking questions like, 'What do you need?' and 'What do you feel?' Allow your inner child to express themselves without judgment. Listen to their responses and offer comfort as the adult protector figure.

I keep a photo of my inner child on my smartwatch so every single day I see her and I'm able to remind her that she is good enough. Our brain works on repetition so you can do the same or even carry a physical photo around of your younger self. This enables you to keep two time lines: back then and now. It helps with unblending you from your inner child so you can recognize you are now an adult.

Reparent your inner child

Reparenting your inner child means taking care of the part of you that holds on to childhood experiences and emotions – your wounded inner child. Below are six simple ways to nurture your inner child as the adult you are now that you can start to implement as a daily practice:

1. Self-compassion

Reflect on your attachment style, your patterns in relationships, and the unresolved emotional wounds from your past. Approach this process with self-compassion, understanding that the wounds you carry are not your fault but the result of your early experiences. Treat yourself with the same kindness and understanding you would offer to a close friend or child. We're often so hard on ourselves, but it's important to step back and look with compassion at the person you are today, having experienced all of this. Be gentle and patient with your feelings and mistakes. Write some affirmations – such as 'I am worthy' – and put them where you'll see them each day, for example on your mirror, giving your younger self that constant reminder. This isn't selfish as many of us may feel, but a necessity. You can't pour from an empty cup.

2. Validate your emotions

Accept and acknowledge your feelings, even if they seem silly or irrational. Your inner child's emotions are valid, and it's OK to feel them. Give yourself space each day to just sit with your emotions and allow them to be seen and heard. This is about not dismissing your emotions, but welcoming them in.

3. Create a safe space

Establish a safe and comforting environment for yourself. This can include a cozy space at home or engaging in activities that make you feel secure. I have an area at home that has candles and a beanbag, where I can cocoon myself and read a book or listen to music. Just to be. Doing nothing is still doing something as we are nurturing our inner child.

4. Take care of your physical and emotional needs

Ensure you eat well, get enough rest, and engage in activities that bring you joy and relaxation. When you're buying food, make sure that you're buying nutritious food, as you would if you were actually feeding your own child. This is so important if neglect was part of your childhood experience.

5. Healing and therapy

Consider talking to a therapist or coach who can help you work through past traumas and childhood issues. Make sure they are trained in somatics so they can work at a nervous system level. Somatic therapy and coaching can provide valuable support in reparenting your inner child and fostering emotional growth.

6. Start to create some intentional daily habits

As children, things can often be chaotic and erratic or even too rigid. Creating some intentional habits that are all about self-love shows your inner child that they matter and belong. Start small and then stack new habits onto existing ones as you're more likely to then stick to them.

Reparenting involves becoming the loving and nurturing caregiver that your inner child needed but may not have had. Imagine yourself as the ideal parent for your inner child, offering unconditional love, validation, and protection. Consistently provide the support and care that was missing during your childhood. This is a vital corrective experience.

Establish boundaries

Setting boundaries with a narcissist can be challenging, but it's a vital step in rebuilding your life after leaving an abusive relationship and is essential for your well-being. Here are 10 simple suggestions to help you get started. First, though, it's important to recognize your intrinsic worth and understand that you deserve respect, safety, and happiness.

1. Identify your boundaries

Clearly understand what you're comfortable with and what you're not. Reflect on your own needs and what makes you feel secure and content. Write down your top values and what would need to happen for these to be pushed. What would be a deal-breaker for you? For instance, if honesty is one of your top values and you feel someone is being dishonest, that is a potential boundary rupture and where strong communication is needed. It's crucial to be specific about your boundaries, whether they pertain to personal space, respect for your opinions, or limits on certain behaviors. Boundaries are about you valuing yourself.

2. Use 'I' statements

Once you've established your boundaries, it's important that you learn to communicate them clearly and directly. Express your feelings and needs using phrases like 'I feel' or 'I need,' rather than blaming or accusing and using 'you.'

3. Stay calm and confident

Approach discussions with confidence and a calm demeanor, even if you don't feel it.

4. Set consequences

Once you've established and communicated a boundary, uphold it firmly. Resist the temptation to compromise or give in to manipulation or guilt. Enforce consequences for those who disregard your boundaries to demonstrate your commitment to maintaining them. Be clear when communicating these consequences. For example, 'If you keep checking my phone, this is a deal-breaker for me, and our relationship will end.'

5. Stick to your limits

Be consistent in enforcing your boundaries, even if they resist.

6. Limit emotional investment

Don't expect them to understand or validate your boundaries; focus on your self-care. They never will.

7. Choose your battles

Prioritize which boundaries are most important and let go of smaller issues.

8. Seek support

Talk to a therapist or someone you trust for guidance and emotional support.

9. Prioritize your physical and emotional well-being

Focus on rebuilding your self-esteem and self-confidence. Recognize your strengths and embrace personal growth as you heal from the scars of narcissistic abuse.

10. Practice extreme modified or no contact

In extreme cases, reducing or cutting off contact with the narcissist may be necessary for your peace of mind, creating emotional and physical distance to protect your healing process. If you have children, consider extreme modified contact (*see page 60 for more on this*).

Remember, setting boundaries with a narcissist can be challenging, but it's essential for your mental and emotional health. Prioritize your well-being and stay firm in your decisions.

Boundaries are not about anyone else, but honoring yourself and your values.

This is a gradual process, and it's OK to take your time. Be patient and kind with yourself, and make your safety, well-being, and recovery top priorities as you move forward.

Boundaries are another expression of self-love and self-respect.

Identify your inner circle

Surround yourself with friends and family who understand and support your healing journey. I call this your emotional ecosystem. Think about the people around you:

- Does everyone get to know everything about you?

- How much time do you devote to a relationship?

- When can you trust someone and let them into your life more?

When asking these questions, it's helpful to think of relationships in terms of circles. Only those who are in your inner circle get access to intimate information about your life. You get to decide which circle a person belongs in when it comes to your life. These people don't need to know where they sit. This is for you to know how much you share with them and how strong your boundaries need to be for each person. Use the diagram opposite to outline who is in what circle in your life.

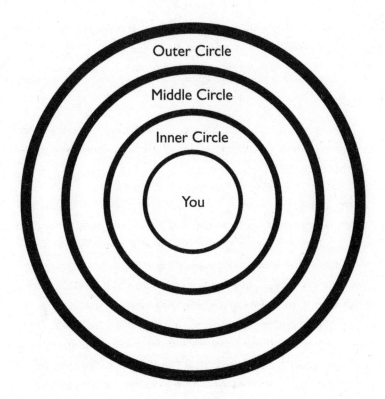

Identify Your Inner Circle

Share your thoughts and feelings with trusted individuals, but also set a time limit on how long you allow yourself to talk about the narcissist – constantly talking about them can make you feel worse as it cements the trauma even more. Once you have mapped out who is in your boundary circles, consider the following questions:

- How did you decide who gets to be in your inner circle?

- Are you in people's inner circle, but they're not in yours?

- When does a person move from one circle to another?

- What kind of information do you share with those in the outer, middle, and inner circles?

- How much time or energy do you spend on a person in the middle and outer circles?

- What are the characteristics of the inner circle people? What is something that would automatically move someone to the outer circle?

Knowing who is in your inner circle of friends and family is essential because they form the nucleus of your support system and play a pivotal role in your emotional well-being. These trusted individuals offer unwavering support, genuine understanding, and unconditional love. They are the ones you can confide in during both joyous moments and challenging times, fostering a sense of belonging and security. An inner circle provides a safe space where you can be your authentic self without judgment, enabling personal growth and emotional resilience. Nurturing these close relationships ensures that you have a reliable foundation of love and trust to navigate life's complexities, making it imperative to cherish and cultivate your inner circle.

Self-care

Engage in regular self-care practices to nurture your physical, emotional, and mental well-being. Some practical examples of this include:

Self-compassion

Practice self-compassion by speaking kindly to yourself. Write down affirmations or positive statements about yourself and repeat these affirmations daily to build self-esteem and self-worth. Focus on nurturing your inner child and soothing any self-doubt or self-blame.

Creative expression

Engage in creative activities like painting, drawing, writing, or crafting. Allow your emotions to flow through your chosen medium. Don't worry about the end result — I'm no artist, but I find this good for the soul. The process of creation is therapeutic. Use your creativity as a way to express and release pent-up emotions.

Physical self-care

Prioritize your physical well-being by getting regular exercise or, if that word scares you, simply move more. Choose activities you enjoy, whether that's yoga, dancing, or walking. Pay attention to your nutrition as the gut plays a huge part in recovery after narcissistic abuse, and aim for balance. Good is better than nothing. Ensure you get enough restful sleep to support your healing process.

Connecting with supportive people

Surround yourself with the inner circle you identified above, but also seek out other social interactions that are positive and uplifting, and maybe start looking for new and engaging hobbies. Avoid or limit contact with people who trigger negative emotions or remind you of the narcissist. You don't get any thanks from anyone for being a martyr.

Therapeutic practices

Consider therapeutic modalities like art therapy, music therapy, or animal-assisted therapy. Work with a therapist trained in trauma and narcissistic abuse recovery, and you can always reach out to me and my team if you need support with this (*see Resources, page 239*). Engage in these therapies as a means to process your emotions and promote healing in nonverbal ways. Collaborate with your therapist to choose the most suitable therapeutic approach for you.

All of these self-care practices can provide valuable support for you after narcissistic abuse during your healing journey. Remember that healing is a unique and ongoing process, so be patient and compassionate with yourself as you implement these strategies.

Mindfulness and grounding techniques

Practicing mindfulness and grounding techniques can help you stay present in the moment and manage overwhelming emotions. These practices are particularly useful when dealing with triggers related to past trauma. We'll discuss more of these in other chapters when we start to explore nervous system regulation, but below are four examples of some really simple techniques that you can start to implement now. These mindfulness and grounding techniques can help you find moments of calm and clarity, getting you back into the green light – the ventral vagal – on the Traffic Lights of Tolerance™ (*see page 67*). Regular practice can contribute to healing and emotional regulation of the nervous system.

5-4-3-2-1 grounding technique

Look around and identify:

- Five things you can see

- Four things you can touch

- Three things you can hear

- Two things you can smell

- One thing you can taste (or imagine tasting)

This technique helps bring your focus to the present moment by engaging your senses.

Box breathing

- Sit or stand comfortably with your back straight.

- Inhale deeply through your nose for a count of four seconds.

- Hold your breath for four seconds.

- Exhale slowly through your mouth for another four seconds.

- Pause and hold your breath again for four seconds.

Repeat this pattern for several rounds, focusing on your breath and the counting. Box breathing helps regulate your nervous system and reduce anxiety.

Body scan meditation

- Find a quiet space, and sit or lie down comfortably.

- Close your eyes and take a few deep breaths.

- Starting at the top of your head, slowly bring your attention down through your body.

- Notice any tension, discomfort, or sensations as you scan each body part.

- Breathe into any areas of tension and imagine them releasing with each exhale.

- Continue scanning and relaxing your entire body.

This practice helps you become more aware of bodily sensations and promotes relaxation.

Mindful walking

- Find a safe and quiet place to walk, indoors or outdoors.

- Begin walking slowly and intentionally, paying attention to each step.

- Notice the sensation of your feet lifting, moving, and making contact with the ground.

- Focus on the rhythm of your steps and your breath.

- If your mind starts to wander, gently bring it back to the sensations of walking.

This practice can help ground you in the present moment and relieve stress.

Surround yourself with supportive relationships

Finding new friendships as an adult can be fulfilling and rewarding, whether in person or online, but I know it can also seem scary and potentially take you right back to the school playground! Go slow, but also know that no one is going to just come knocking on your door – you have to be intentional. We're wired for connection as humans, but I know how easy it can be to isolate ourselves. I always say, had it not been for my children, I would have easily become agoraphobic.

In person, consider exploring your local community by participating in events, classes, or groups related to your interests. Attend workshops, join a fitness class, or engage in a hobby club. For example, if you're into photography, look for local photography clubs or workshops in your area. Attend these gatherings regularly, strike up conversations, and be open to forming connections with those who share your passion.

Online platforms like Facebook can also be a valuable resource for making new friends. To start, you can search for groups that align with your interests or hobbies. Join those where people discuss topics you're passionate about, whether that's gardening, cooking, book clubs, or fitness. You can even join my free Facebook group (see *Resources, page 239*). Engage in conversations by commenting on posts, sharing your experiences, and asking questions. As you become more active in these groups, you'll likely encounter like-minded individuals. Don't hesitate to reach out through private messages to establish deeper connections and suggest meeting up in person if they live nearby. I have lots of people in my community who have made some amazing friends doing this.

Another effective online approach is to use social media to reconnect with old friends and acquaintances or to expand your network. You can reach out to former classmates, colleagues, or people from your hometown. Sharing updates, commenting on their posts, and expressing genuine interest in their lives can rekindle old connections and potentially lead to new friendships. Remember, whether in person or online, the key to forming lasting friendships is to be open, approachable, and genuinely interested in getting to know others.

Building a network of supportive friends and loved ones who can offer understanding and empathy can provide corrective experiences that counterbalance the negative effects of narcissistic relationships. Start to name people who you actually want to be around and rid yourself of the dementors sucking the life force out of you. Who you surround yourself with is so important.

Journaling and expression

Starting a journaling practice can be a rewarding and effective way to express your thoughts, emotions, and experiences. I used to hate journaling, but that was because I was setting myself up for failure as my expectation was too high. To set yourself up for success, follow these simple pointers:

1. Choose the right time

Pick a consistent time that works for you. It could be in the morning to reflect on the day ahead or in the evening to unwind and process your thoughts. Find a time when you can focus without distractions.

2. Determine frequency

Decide how often you want to journal. Starting with just a few times a week is perfectly fine. It's essential to make it manageable and sustainable for you. You can always increase the frequency as you become more comfortable.

3. Select your stationery

Opt for a journal or notebook that you enjoy writing in. This really helped me – I love stationery so I bought a nice journal and pen. Whether it's a classic leather-bound journal, a colorful notebook, or a digital journaling app, choose something that appeals to you. Ensure you have a pen or a device with a comfortable keyboard if you prefer digital journaling.

4. Create a comfortable space

Find a quiet and comfortable spot where you can write without interruptions. This can be at your desk, in a cozy chair, or even outdoors if that's where you feel most inspired. I like writing at bedtime in my bed as it feels the best time and space for me.

5. Set a reasonable goal

Start with a manageable goal for each journaling session. It could be writing for just 3–5 minutes. Avoid putting pressure on yourself to write lengthy entries. This was my downfall to start with as I thought I needed to be like everyone else. But who is everyone else?

6. Begin with a prompt

If you're unsure what to write about, begin with a prompt or question. It can be as simple as 'How was your day?' or 'What are you grateful for today?' This can help get the words flowing. Gratitude is my favorite daily practice (see *page 148 for more on this*).

7. Write freely

Don't worry about grammar, spelling, or structure. Write freely and honestly, letting your thoughts flow onto the page. Remember, it's for your eyes only, so there's no need to be perfect.

8. Reflect and review

Periodically, take time to review your journal entries. This can help you gain insights into your thoughts and emotions over time and track your personal growth.

By following these steps, you can establish a successful journaling practice that aligns with your schedule and preferences. The key is to make it an enjoyable and reflective experience, free from pressure or expectations.

Embrace growth and resilience

Healing is not a linear process; it involves setbacks and challenges. Embrace the growth and resilience you develop along the way. Each step forward is a victory in itself. All of the above steps are invitational as you may find some easier than others. Lean into that and explore why this may be the case. It's vital that you do act upon these exercises, though, otherwise your inner child will keep ruling how you act in the present.

Inner child healing is a profound journey of self-discovery and self-compassion. All healing is actually self-healing – coming back to a place where you know you are good enough simply by being you. By addressing attachment wounds, shame, and engaging in corrective attachment experiences, as outlined in the steps above, you can transform your relationship with yourself and others, meaning the more destructive and exhausting protector responses can calm in the system.

As you reparent your inner child, establish healthy boundaries, and practice self-care, you create a brighter future filled with the potential for healthier, more fulfilling relationships. Healing your inner child is an empowering process that enables you to break free from the patterns of the past, transform your somatic experience of childhood, and ultimately thrive and step into post-traumatic growth.

You are enough; you were then, you
are now, and you always will be.

In the next chapter, I'm going to share some somatic experiencing techniques and trauma healing. If at any stage it feels too much, stop. Consult your healthcare provider if you feel you're in any doubt.

Healing needs to happen at the pace of your nervous system. I know it can feel like a slow process, but, as I've said, the key to building a flexible nervous system is to go slowly – known as titration. By doing so, you'll have longer-lasting processing and integration. If a frustrated part of you comes up, acknowledge and honor it, but let it know the reason you're going slow. Parts need to be heard, so always unbend and try to let them know that you thank them for wanting to help, but you've got this.

CHAPTER 6

Moving from Freeze to Thaw

True healing comes through getting to know our protector response and then helping our nervous system work safely and slowly through the hierarchy and the Traffic Lights of Tolerance™. The importance of reclaiming yourself and feeling safe in your body at a nervous system level cannot be overstated. You can create a safe home environment, but if you still feel unsafe in your body, you'll stay activated and dysregulated. This process involves delving deep into your inner self, acknowledging past traumas and narcissistic abuse, and establishing a profound sense of security. When we achieve this, we unlock a world of physical and mental well-being that can positively impact every facet of our lives, leading to post-traumatic growth.

As we explored in Chapter 4, when we have experienced narcissistic abuse in a world filled with stressors, expectations, and constant stimuli, many of us will be stuck in a freeze response – the red of the Traffic Lights of Tolerance™. We can feel disconnected from our own body – known as dissociation – and often merely functioning. Most of the people I work with who have experienced narcissistic abuse have dissociation as one of their protector responses. This is often interspersed with explosive moments of anger, when we scan for danger, moving us into the sympathetic yellow light. We then often feel shame because anger in the Western world means that people may judge us, think we are weak, or even like the abuser. This means we don't process the anger, and instead we suppress and shut it down again. So many people get stuck between red and yellow because, though the body will try hard to start to heal, as a society we haven't learned how to express healthy rage and anger, so we put a lid on it and back down into red we go. It's like a pan of boiling water that we're jamming a lid on – the water is boiling, but we won't allow it to overflow. The problem with this is that we stay stuck, and this is what can lead to long-term chronic illness and disease.

Every single experience we've had will have a cycle and we may move through the traffic lights all the time – we call this a flexible nervous system. We can often notice when people complete a response cycle as they might shake or cry and then let out a huge exhale as the body comes back into the present and grounds. Think about those animals that shake off their energy after something dangerous. As humans, though, we often overthink and suppress that, and this is where the protector response comes in. It's stopping you from completing the response cycle to come back to that green light, our social engagement system, the ventral vagal.

To heal from narcissistic abuse, we need to know how to move from freeze, through sympathetic fight and flight – and discharge that anger in a healthy way – to thaw into the green light and feel safe, present, grounded, and connected again. The regulation techniques in this chapter will show you how to do just that so you can regulate your emotions better. This doesn't mean we'll never feel the challenges of life again; what it means is that you'll have a bigger capacity to cope and a greater awareness.

Some people may find the following techniques too much, so just listen to your body and, if they're not enjoyable or cause you more activation, stop. Again, the key is to go in a much more titrated way. Even trying these techniques for two minutes will enable you to track and see what sensations you notice in your body.

*Slowing down actually speeds up
your healing in the long run.*

NERVOUS SYSTEM REGULATION

Reclaiming yourself and feeling safe within your body begins with a process known as nervous system regulation. Think back to your own IFS with your true self and your exile inner child wound (see *Chapter 3*). When we don't feel safe simply to be ourselves, we adapt to our surroundings to stay safe. Nervous system regulation helps us build a flexible nervous system so that we can navigate the challenges of narcissistic abuse and life by not going into a constant trauma and survival response. This means we need to build capacity in our nervous system so that we can cope.

It's crucial to note that the process of reclaiming yourself and regulating the nervous system is not a quick fix, but a lifelong journey. Healing is not a destination. It requires patience, self-compassion, and a commitment to self-care. It involves creating a safe and nurturing environment, both internally and externally. When you feel safe within your own body, you're better equipped to handle life's challenges and thrive in your personal and professional life.

Moving from Freeze (Red Light) to Fight/Flight (Yellow Light)

There are two different types of freeze: the high and low dorsal tone. The high tone is uneasiness. For instance, I was in freeze most of the time, but equally I couldn't concentrate or sit still. If I watched television, I was constantly flicking through the channels. My focus just wasn't there. This often happens when C-PTSD is present as the volume of the amygdala, your fear center, increases in size and the hippocampus (responsible for learning and memory) starts to shrink, which is why so many of us suffer with brain fog and memory loss. The good news is this can be reversed.

Low dorsal tone is when you are in shutdown and have zero energy at all. I dipped between these two states all the time, both during my marriage to my ex-husband and for a number of years after. If we're constantly stuck in freeze, then to heal we need to go into the sympathetic nervous system, but this can be a scary place for many, often bringing up feelings of 'What if people judge me?', 'What if people think I'm weak?', 'What if people think I can't cope?'

In the wild, freeze is a biological response to danger where the animal feigns death or gets really small so the predator doesn't see them. It's never the animal giving up, just trying to stay alive. The fight-or-flight response means getting bigger to fight the predator or to mobilize all that energy to flee and get to safety.

If you think about yourself, freeze is actually your best friend when you're in a relationship with a narcissist and trying to heal, as your nervous system wants to keep you small, invisible, because at least then you're alive and the safest you can be. If you're invisible, surely no one can hurt you? You may know cognitively that you don't want to stay there, but your nervous system focuses on survival, which is the primary action for us as human beings. In order to heal, though, we have to move through the hierarchy and discharge that sympathetic energy. We must complete the trauma response cycle, even though it may feel unsafe.

At this stage, you need to prioritize self-care and stress-reduction techniques, such as mindfulness, meditation, and deep breathing exercises, to help regulate the body's stress response and tone the vagus nerve. Before we look at some of these techniques, it's important that you understand how your brain operates under stress.

The brain under stress

When we go into a state of arousal because our body has detected danger or, as we know with narcissistic abuse, perceived danger (because the narcissist is triggering all our inner child wounds), our brain moves from executive functioning in our neocortex, the front part of the brain, and being 'online,' to shifting and going 'offline,' into our limbic system, the emotional part of the brain. The image overleaf shows researcher Dr. Daniel Siegel's 'Hand Model of the Brain.'[1] This is a great way to explain these mental processes. Siegel made a distinction between the limbic system, which is in charge of creating emotions, memories, and interpersonal connections, and the cortex, which is the most recently developed part of the brain and is in charge of thinking and reasoning. The limbic system is the oldest and most primitive part of the brain, controlling automatic body functions like breathing, heartbeat, and the fight-or-flight response. The limbic brain area frequently takes precedence over the neocortex when we become anxious, leading to the sensation of 'flipping your lid.' Your environment becomes disorganized and inflexible in this state.[2]

If you put your thumb in the middle of your palm and then fold your fingers over the top, you'll have a model of your brain.

Eyes

Back of head

Your eyes are in front of the knuckles. The back of your head is toward the back of the hand.

Cortex

The top of the brain is called the cortex, represented by your four fingers.

The brain is connected to the rest of the body through the spinal cord, represented by your wrist.

Spinal cord

Hand Model of the Brain

Imagine your brain is like a fist. The lower part of your hand, which is your palm and fingers, represents the calm and thinking part of your brain. This is where you can make good choices, solve problems, and feel happy. Your thumb is like the emotional and reactive part of your brain, the limbic system. When you're really upset or angry, it's like the 'lid' of your hand flips, and your thumb takes over. This can make you act without thinking and sometimes not make good choices. We have gone 'offline,' as opposed to staying 'online' in the rational and logical part of the brain.

The goal when it comes to healing after narcissistic abuse is to keep your 'lid' down so you can use the thinking and calm part of your brain. When something really big and emotional happens and you flip your lid, it's essential to flip the lid back down, to get back 'online' and let the thinking part of your brain take over again, so you can make better decisions and feel better.

In simple terms, it's like having a hand that can think and a thumb that can feel strong emotions. We want to use both but make sure the thinking part is in control most of the time.

Trying to get resolution when you're in your limbic system and the other person is also in their limbic system is nigh on impossible. This is why it's so important to recognize that you can't communicate effectively with a narcissist – they're always offline as they're wounded individuals, so even if you're more rational, they will always be waiting to 'win.'

When we're offline, we've usually gone back to a different time line in our life. Imagine you're in your green light, the ventral vagal part of your nervous system. You have an exchange with the narcissist and you feel all these sensations come up in your body. You were 'online' in the present, feeling safe, and then all of a sudden, you perceive danger. The narcissist is reminding you of a past inner child wound and your nervous system reacts. The amygdala, which is in your limbic system and is your fear center, wants to protect you so you go offline and your nervous system is activated to protect you. You may also have an anger part come up, or even a dissociation part, to protect you from the pain you may have started to feel in that moment. You have gone back to the original time line of when the wound was formed because you have not had any disconfirming or corrective experiences for this not to happen – your nervous system is stuck in that time line.

Meditation, mindfulness and, indeed, all the nervous system regulation techniques I will share, try to help you get back 'online' and into the present moment as the adult you are, not the child you were when you are 'offline.'

Mindfulness and meditation

One effective method for regulating the nervous system and fostering a sense of safety within one's body is through mindfulness and meditation. These techniques allow you to tune in to your bodily sensations, emotions, and thoughts without judgment. By cultivating self-awareness, you can begin to identify areas of tension, unresolved traumas, and triggers that keep your nervous systems in a state of arousal.

Daily meditation has gained widespread attention due to its numerous proven benefits for mental and physical well-being. Research has shown that incorporating a regular meditation practice into one's daily routine can have profound effects on various aspects of human health and cognition.[3] Studies have consistently demonstrated that daily meditation reduces stress and anxiety.[4] Meditation practices promote relaxation by calming the sympathetic nervous system, which is responsible for the 'fight-or-flight' response. Regular meditation also leads to lower levels of the stress hormone cortisol, contributing to a more peaceful and balanced state of mind.

Additionally, daily meditation has been associated with improved emotional regulation and increased self-awareness. Research shows that it enhances gray matter density in brain regions responsible for memory, learning, and self-awareness.[5] This leads to better concentration, enhanced cognitive abilities, and greater emotional resilience.

Moreover, meditation positively impacts physical health. Regular practice has been linked to lowered blood pressure, improved immune function, and reduced inflammation, all of which contribute to a healthier overall lifestyle. Now you can see why I'm such an advocate of meditation!

Meditation

Meditation is a practice that can promote relaxation, mindfulness, and mental well-being. I used to struggle with meditation as my mind would be all over the place, but with regular practice, I now do 20 minutes every day – it's like flexing a muscle. To get you started, here are my top tips:

1. Begin by finding a quiet and comfortable place where you won't be disturbed. You can sit on a chair, cushion, or the floor. Make sure your back is straight but not rigid, and your hands can rest on your lap or knees. You may also want to lie down – this is my preference.

2. Decide how long you want to meditate for. For beginners, start with just 3–5 minutes per session. As you become more comfortable, you can gradually increase the duration to 10–20 minutes or longer if you wish. Use a timer or meditation app to keep track of the time. This way, you won't have to worry about checking the clock during your meditation.

3. Close your eyes gently and focus on your breath. Breathe naturally and pay attention to the sensation of the breath entering and leaving your nostrils or the rise and fall of your chest or abdomen. Placing your hands on your heart and stomach helps ensure you are doing deep belly breaths.

4. Observe your thoughts. As you meditate, thoughts may arise. This is normal. Instead of trying to push them away, observe them without judgment, like clouds passing by. Then, gently bring your attention back to your breath.

5. Practice regularly – consistency is key. Aim to meditate daily, especially if you're a beginner. Over time, meditation becomes more comfortable, and you'll reap greater benefits from regular practice.

6. There are various meditation techniques to explore, such as mindfulness, loving kindness (see *page 141*), or body scan meditation (see *page 101*). Experiment with different approaches to find what resonates with you best.

7. Be patient. Meditation is a skill that develops with time. Don't be discouraged if your mind wanders; it's a natural part of the process. Just return to your breath or chosen focal point.

8. If you're new to meditation, consider guided meditation sessions or apps that offer audio guidance. These can be helpful in providing structure and instruction.

Remember, meditation is a personal practice, and there's no one-size-fits-all approach. Adjust the details to suit your comfort and preferences, and, most importantly, be patient and kind to yourself as you develop your meditation practice over time.

Mindfulness

A great mindfulness technique is what I call the 'Comfort Router Box.' Find a nice box and put things that represent all five senses into it. For my box, I have:

- Sight: A photo of my two children and my mother.

- Smell: An aroma ball that smells so wonderful and I immediately feel a sense of calm when smelling it.

- Sound: A Post-it note reminding me of three Spotify playlists that I have – 80s music, 90s dance (don't judge me!), and a ventral vagal playlist filled with my favorite classical music.

- Touch: A black stone that I got in Mexico years ago that has such wonderful memories attached to it, but is also smooth and cold to touch, and really engages this sense.

- Taste: A small chocolate that I can mindfully eat and savor the taste of.

We cannot biologically engage our senses and stay offline in our limbic system. This exercise moves us more online and into the here and now as the senses become engaged. I would even suggest that the whole family creates a Comfort Router Box so that, if you see someone else in your family going 'offline,' you can lovingly offer the box to them as their router to get back online. This is a great, fun activity to do with children and an ideal opportunity to talk to them about emotions, feelings, and their nervous system. Remember, there are no bad feelings or bad parts; they're all just protecting you from your perception and interpretation of something. Imagine if you'd learned that at school!

Breathwork practice and breathing techniques

Incorporating breathing exercises into your daily routine is a powerful tool for nervous system regulation. Deep, diaphragmatic breathing activates the ventral vagal part of our nervous system, signaling to the body that it's safe to relax. Regular practice of deep breathing can reduce the physical and emotional symptoms of chronic stress, such as muscle tension, anxiety, and racing thoughts, and we can then step into post-traumatic growth and live our best life.

We hear a lot about breathwork, and I use it on a daily basis, but there are also breathing techniques, and the two are different.

Breathwork

Breathing is one of the only systems in our body that can be both conscious and unconscious – you're not thinking about breathing right now, but you're still doing it – and we can focus on our breathing and bring in good breathwork practice. But why do we even need a good breathwork practice? Surely if we do this unconsciously, it should just happen? Unfortunately, it's not as simple as that. When we're in a trauma response, we tend to breathe shallowly in the upper part of our chest, almost like we're holding our breath.

Stop and take a moment to notice your breathing right now. Is it deep into your belly or is it shallow in the upper part of your chest? If it's shallow, it's because your body is in a preparatory response for potential threat, which is totally understandable after narcissistic abuse. If you were being chased by a lion, you wouldn't be doing deep belly breaths, would you? Instead, you would be running away and breathing shallowly in a sympathetic response to get to safety.

Unfortunately, we do the same when the narcissist is there, even though we're not in actual danger – remember, that's our perception because our version of danger is feeling those negative beliefs about ourselves. Also notice if you have a clenched jaw or raised shoulders. If you do, try unclenching your jaw, dropping your shoulders, and doing a belly breath. What do you start to notice in your body?

Breathwork is about helping our body, with conscious deep breathing, to get back to a state of presence so we can adopt a more natural breathing state.

Using a 5-2-8 breathwork practice can really help you calm your nervous system in the moment, when you bring awareness to the fact that you're living in a trauma response. You breathe in through your nose for a count of five, then hold the count for two and then exhale for eight. By extending the exhale by three counts, you are, in essence, tricking your body into the feeling of being safe. I use this breathwork practice all the time as it really helps me downregulate and puts me in a lovely state of presence and safety. Try it, and notice what you feel in your body. It may feel strange at first and, if it feels too much, stop and come back to it another time.

Some people find breathwork too triggering, so be mindful with your practice and start to learn to listen to your body as you have likely been disconnected for many years, decades in my case.

Breathing techniques

While breathwork practice is working on the here and the now to get you back to feeling safe, breathing techniques are something entirely different. Breathing techniques can help us mobilize energy in our nervous system to help us start to process and integrate past trauma into our body, so we can feel safe as the adult we are today. As we've seen, most of you will be in a freeze response, but will likely have moments of explosive anger, only to suppress that for fear of judgment and dissociate again. But to truly move from freeze to thaw, we have to move from the red to the yellow light and actually discharge this energy to then move to the green, the ventral vagal part of our nervous system.

There are many people in my community who have moved into the sympathetic, through something like exercise, but their body doesn't recognize that this sympathetic is a positive sympathetic – it just thinks it's dangerous, that they will appear bigger and more visible to the narcissist, so they shut back down and freeze again, and this cycle can keep happening.

The Voo breathing technique helps to send a signal – known as afferent neurons – from the gut to the brain that you are here and in the present, not back in the danger. With regular practice, it helps tone the vagus nerve and the more we tone it, the better the ability we have to navigate the weight of any stressful situations as we have a bigger capacity to cope.

To do the Voo breathing technique, inhale in through the nose, then make a 'Voo' sound when you exhale, like a foghorn, opening your mouth until you just reach a resistance and are making a foghorn-like sound, reverberating from your belly through to your throat. Doing this 8–10 times a few times a day can really help bring some gentle energy into the sympathetic part of the nervous system that can feel safer to work with initially. It will also help tone that ventral vagal part of the nervous system that, if you remember, may never have been taught to you as a child.

You may feel super silly doing this, but it's a fantastic breathing technique on so many levels and I use it so much when I'm working with my clients. Dr. Peter Levine, who founded one of the best trauma therapies out there, called somatic experiencing, created this technique and it's widely used among practitioners.[6]

Moving from Fight/Flight (Yellow Light) to Safe (Green Light)

How many times have you felt like you could explode and then felt shame? This is actually a great sign of healing because it shows you may have moved from freeze into flight/flight and your nervous system felt safe to do so. But how do we healthily discharge this pent-up energy in our body without shouting at our children or punching a wall? This was the hardest part for me on my healing journey as I had associated aggression with abuse, perpetrators, not coping, and weakness. I had been brought up with the idea that little girls should be seen and not heard, and I had learned that emotions were bad. As I hope you have now come to understand, this is not true.

Emotions are there for a reason; sensations
are there for a reason. They are not bad.

This may also be the hardest step for you as so much shame can show up here, pushing you back down into freeze. Please know, though, that feeling an anger or rage part in this process is normal. You have been abused. Maybe you were heavily let down in your childhood. None of this is your fault. Read these words again slowly: THIS IS NOT YOUR FAULT. However, it *is* your responsibility to self-heal as, sadly, no one is coming to rescue you. To really start to heal and see some true, long-lasting shifts, give yourself this gift and rescue yourself.

The techniques below will show you how to release, rather than suppress, the fight/flight sympathetic energy to then feel more present and grounded in the ventral vagal system and the green light. The tears may start to flow as you finally give yourself space to feel and let them come. Tears are designed to help regulate our nervous system and tears from emotion actually have a hormone in them to do this, so let them flow. Crying is good. If we don't cry and release, we internalize all of this and this is then when chronic illness shows up.

How to discharge sympathetic energy

* Hold a rolled-up towel horizontally with your hands at each end. Slowly twisting the towel can help to release this energy. It engages the shoulders, where a lot of the charge can be held, and you can even add in your voice and words. You may want to say things to the narcissist that you may never actually say to them. The brain can't distinguish between the past and the present when it comes to processing emotions and trauma. Just because you may have suppressed your impulses throughout your relationship with the narcissist, as it may have been unsafe to say anything, it doesn't mean the impulse wasn't there. When we honor that impulse, the brain just thinks we

have now completed that trauma response cycle. You can also add in a slight change to the Voo breath here. Breathe as per the exercise above, but change 'Voo' to 'Voo Ah' – really go for it and twist the towel. Notice that you may keep taking bigger breaths; you may even start to yawn, have stomach gurgles, burp, or fart – these are all signs of processing.

• Try pushing against a wall. Set your stance in a shallow lunge position and place your hands on the wall. Visualize pushing all the sympathetic energy into the wall and, again, use your voice. If there are people around you, visualize yourself shouting or screaming – you can still get deep results, even if it's in your head. I remember doing this exercise at a healing event I held, and I had everyone on the wall around the room. The air was blue – there was shouting, there were tears, but it was electric and such a beautiful corrective experience as everyone felt seen and heard from, releasing what had been suppressed for years.

Now you're releasing some of this sympathetic energy, you can hopefully start to step into feeling more present and in the ventral vagal part of your nervous system. But how do you stay there and continue to keep honing your vagus nerve, increasing your capacity, and building a more flexible nervous system that can get stretched but not stressed?

Staying in the Ventral Vagal (Green Light)

If we think back to our nervous system as a hierarchy, the ventral vagal is where we would like to remain the majority of the time. We'll still need elements of the sympathetic nervous system (to exercise, for example) and the dorsal vagal (to really relax, perhaps in a lovely bubble bath), so it's important not to just think of the nervous system purely for trauma – we need all aspects of it daily. However, we want to try to stay present and tone the vagus nerve.

Some of the ways I tone my vagus nerve on a daily basis include:

- Gratitude practice (see page 148)

- Meditation (see page 117)

- Ice bath: I have an ice bath in my back garden set to 11°C. I get in it every morning for eight minutes. This helps tone my vagus nerve as I get used to being in an uncomfortable situation, and trains my body to know that I can be uncomfortable and still be in control and safe

- Breathwork: I bring in breathing techniques like those on page 122 if I'm feeling tired, to mobilize energy

- Towel work: I do the towel work exercise on page 124 if I feel an anger part

- Parts journaling (see below)

This is my daily practice to keep increasing my nervous system capacity. Each year, my healing goes deeper, and I'm better able to cope with any of life's challenges, even after the narcissistic abuse.

Parts journaling

Parts journaling is a valuable tool for understanding and managing our thoughts and emotions, helping us stay in the ventral vagal part of our nervous system. When we write down our feelings and thoughts, we give our different inner parts a chance to express themselves. By doing this, we can identify what makes us feel calm and safe, and what might trigger stress or anxiety. It's like having a map to navigate our emotions.

Grab a notebook or a piece of paper and a pen. At the top of the page, write down the name of the part that is showing up. Then, below this, journal on the following:

- Its age, gender and appearance

- Your feelings toward this part

- Any physical sensations you feel/the location of the part

- What is its job?

- What does it need you to know?

When we know what's going on inside us, we can make choices that keep us in that calm and safe ventral vagal state, making us feel more at ease and in control of our reactions to life's challenges. Parts journaling is a way to keep checking in on our parts – it's like a compass guiding us toward a more peaceful and balanced state of mind. Try it and see what impact it has for you.

STOP APOLOGIZING AND START THANKING

The words you use have a profound impact on how you end up feeling. Chronic over-apologizing can have a significant negative effect upon the brain as it keeps you in a state of scarcity instead of abundance. As we've explored, the brain's job is to keep you safe and in a state of what's familiar. It doesn't recognize whether it's right or wrong, it just acts upon what YOU tell it. This means that you have tremendous power.

Simply changing and tweaking some sentences that you would normally say to yourself can have a huge impact because, rather than firing negative neurons in the brain, it fires positive ones.

Try switching your language and saying to yourself:

- 'Thank you for being accepting of me.'
- 'Thank you for being patient when I make a mistake.'
- 'Thank you for listening to me.'
- 'Thank you for waiting for me.'

Rather than coming from a place of apology, we're coming from a place of gratitude, and this will greatly increase your levels of well-being. You have so much power over your mind with the words you choose to tell it, so choose wisely.

Nervous system mapping

Use the table below to create your own nervous system map to explore how you can shift from the red light into yellow and then into green, and stay there. This exercise is an adaptation of Deb Dana's ladder.[7] It works really well with children too. It's split into two aspects: what you can do on your own to self-regulate and what you can do with others to co-regulate.

	Things I can do on my own	Things I can do with others
Red light: freeze, dorsal vagal	*What moves me out of here?*	*What moves me out of here?*
Yellow light: fight/ flight, sympathetic	*What moves me out of here?*	*What moves me out of here?*
Green light: safe, ventral vagal	*What helps me stay here?*	*What helps me stay here?*

This can be your somatic bible to support your nervous system as you navigate your healing after narcissistic abuse. Keep doing this every day for the rest of your life, as this will not only help you emotionally but also physically in the long run.

When the body isn't in a constant state of fight/flight or freeze, it can prioritize essential functions such as digestion, immune response, and tissue repair. This can lead to improved overall health and a reduced risk of chronic illnesses. Now you can see why I say the narcissist woke me up! Had I not done this work, I dread to think what effect this would have had on my long-term health, especially when I think about my mother, who died at the age of 67 – so young.

In the realm of relationships, the importance of reclaiming yourself at a nervous system level cannot be understated. When you're secure within your own body and emotions, you're better able to form healthy, loving connections with others. You can communicate more effectively, set boundaries, and engage in more fulfilling relationships. This doesn't mean you'll have a life without challenges, but within those challenges, your nervous system will feel present and safe, and won't constantly take you back to childhood experiences. Healing isn't about never feeling activated again; it's about bringing in faster awareness and then having the tools to do something about it. So, while this book is about healing after narcissistic abuse, the tools are for you to use for the rest of your life and to share with others.

The journey of reclaiming yourself and feeling safe within your body at a nervous system level is a profound and transformative process. It's a path to improved mental and physical health, enriched relationships, and a greater overall quality of life. In a world filled with constant stressors, finding safety within yourself is not a luxury but a necessity. Learning to regulate your emotions in the present is a lifelong skill — there will always be times in our life when we can feel activated — and it means we can recognize these sensations and catch them before they flood the nervous system. When we can regulate ourselves like this, we can continue to heal at a deeper level.

In the next chapter, I'll introduce you to the transformative tools of positive psychology. By prioritizing self-care, self-awareness, and self-healing, you can embark on this journey of self-reclamation and unlock the true potential of your mind and body. It's a journey that, once begun, can lead to a life filled with greater peace, joy, and resilience.

CHAPTER 7

The Power of Positive Psychology

You established a foundation of nervous system regulation in the last chapter. It's now time to look to the future and explore how you can deepen your understanding. This is where positive psychology comes in.

Integrating positive psychology with trauma-informed practice is vital for our recovery, and it's something I do every day – I almost can't imagine one without the other. You can't lead your best life unless you heal your past, and you don't want to constantly stay stuck in your past as you'll miss the joy of life in the present. Embracing positive psychology means we take it one step further – we don't just bounce back, we bounce *forward*.

This is why I created my School of Trauma-Informed Positive Psychology – I'm focused on integrating these two pieces together as I believe this will accelerate healing the past so you can live a better future. The synergy of positive psychology interventions with nervous system regulation is profound. Nervous system regulation sets the stage by creating a physiological environment conducive to emotional self-healing. Practicing nervous system regulation techniques helps calm the nervous system, making you far more receptive to positive psychology interventions.

Furthermore, positive psychology interventions provide you with the psychological tools to counteract shame's negative impact on your self-esteem and self-worth. The self-compassion, strength-based approaches, and gratitude practices that we'll explore in this chapter offer new ways of thinking and relating to oneself. They help you build emotional resilience and a more realistic and positive self-concept. The amalgamation of these approaches allows you to address the shame of narcissistic abuse and fosters lasting change and personal growth.

The following exercises and interventions are designed for you to reenvision your future with all the possibilities that you can now start to see are available to you. They all elevate your healing by using evidence-based techniques. In other words, if you do the following and commit to them, you'll notice a shift in happiness and well-being because they have been researched and proven.[1]

Self-Compassion

It starts with self-compassion. This is a cornerstone of positive psychology interventions. It involves treating oneself with the same kindness and understanding that one would offer to a friend. Dr. Kristin Neff, a pioneering researcher in self-compassion, suggests that practicing self-compassion can significantly reduce shame.[2] It involves self-kindness, common humanity (recognizing that everyone makes mistakes), and mindfulness (acknowledging one's feelings without judgment). By integrating self-compassion exercises into your daily routines, you can counteract the harsh self-criticism that shame often instigates.

An audio to your inner best friend

One of the exercises I ask my clients to do if they start to feel an inner critic part showing up is to step into self-compassion and send an audio to themselves as if they were speaking to their best friend – with kindness and compassion. This helps unblend the part and give perspective. I'd like you to try it now too. Grab a piece of A4 paper and a pen and write down 30 things you're good at, from the 'I' perspective. For example:

- 'I'm a good parent.'

- 'I'm a great tennis player.'

- 'I'm good at knitting'

- 'I'm an excellent cook.'

Once you've written all 30 things down, I want you to record yourself reading this list three times. Each time you list your strengths and virtues, it allows you to see yourself with so much more kindness. As survivors of narcissistic abuse, we often self-abuse because that's what we are used to feeling like. This exercise helps minimize that.

Self-care vision board

If you've spent years internally putting yourself down, this exercise will feel alien to start off with. You have to keep doing the nervous system work from the last chapter or your self-sabotaging part will just keep coming up for you.

The task at hand entails making a vision board for self-care. You might be used to creating a goal board, often with material items, but this takes it to a more personal and self-healing level.

A vision board uses words, photos, and/or graphics to visually portray a certain idea. Consequently, a self-care vision board is an assortment of pictures and words that represent self-care concepts. You engage in self-care practices to look after your physical, mental, and emotional well-being. To develop your vision board for self-care, follow the four steps below:

1. Come up with self-care options: Make a list of all the potential self-care activities you can think of. Be brave and imaginative, allowing yourself to think of novel and unconventional possible activities. Only activities that meet your values, lifestyle, and level of enjoyment should be listed.

2. Gather pictures for your vision board: Choose uplifting photos that go with the self-care practices you have chosen. Look for pictures that speak to and motivate you. Consider using the internet, magazines, and pictures as prospective sources. Use pictures of things you can do to better look after yourself and your needs. Creating a self-care vision board with images that reflect your commitment to self-care practices can be a powerful way to visualize your goals and inspire self-care.

3. Gather terms for your vision board: You have the option of adding words and phrases to your vision board or keeping it entirely visual. The words and phrases you select should relate to or reflect the self-care practices you have selected. You might prefer to print words from the internet or cut them out of print publications. Pick typefaces and words that speak to and inspire you.

4. Create your vision board: Get creative with your layout once you have gathered your photographs and motivational quotes.

Examples for your self-care vision board

Self-care activities

The following self-care activities can be integrated easily into your busy life and offer quick ways to improve your self-esteem and overall well-being:

- Deep breathing exercise: Find a quiet moment, even if it's just a few minutes. Close your eyes and take a deep breath in through your nose for a count of four. Hold your breath for a count of four. Exhale slowly through your mouth for a count of four. Repeat this cycle a few times to calm your mind and reduce stress.

- Positive affirmations: Stand in front of a mirror and look at yourself. Say three positive affirmations out loud, such as 'I am worthy,' 'I am capable,' or 'I am loved.' Believe in the words you say to boost your self-esteem.

- Take a 10-minute walk: During a break at work or any free moment, step outside. Walk briskly for just 10 minutes, feeling the fresh air and focusing on your surroundings. Physical activity and a change of scenery can lift your mood.

- Journal: Set aside a few minutes each day, maybe before bedtime. Write down three things you're grateful for. Then, jot down one positive thing you accomplished or experienced during the day. Reflecting on positives can improve your self-perception.

- Listen to music: Whenever you have a moment, put on your favorite uplifting song. Close your eyes and let the music wash over you. Allow yourself to feel the emotions the music brings. Music can be a quick mood booster and a form of self-expression.

Pictures

- Nature and serenity: Look for images of serene natural landscapes like beaches, forests, or mountains. *Examples: a tranquil sunset over the ocean, a peaceful forest path, or a serene mountain lake.* These images represent the importance of connecting with nature for relaxation.

- Mindfulness and meditation: Find pictures that capture the essence of mindfulness and meditation. *Examples: images of people meditating, practicing yoga, or simply sitting in quiet reflection.* These visuals symbolize your commitment to inner peace and mental well-being.

- Healthy eating: Search for images of nourishing and wholesome foods that support a balanced diet. *Examples: fresh fruits and vegetables, colorful salads, or a beautifully arranged breakfast bowl.* These pictures remind you to prioritize nutritious eating habits.

- Physical activity and movement: Look for photos that represent various forms of movement. *Examples: images of people jogging, practicing yoga, or hiking in the great outdoors.* These visuals signify your dedication to maintaining a healthy body.

- Relaxation and self-care rituals: Find pictures that depict relaxing activities and self-care routines. *Examples: pictures of spa treatments, hot baths with candles, or cozy reading nooks.* These images symbolize your commitment to pampering yourself.

- Positive affirmations: Include images that feature uplifting and motivating words. *Examples: visuals with phrases like 'You are enough,' 'Self-care is self-love,' or 'I prioritize my well-being.'* These affirmations reinforce your self-care commitment.

- Quality time with loved ones: Look for pictures that capture moments of connection with family and friends. *Examples: images of people sharing laughter, hugging, or enjoying quality time together.* These visuals highlight the importance of nurturing relationships.

- Restful sleep: Find images that represent restful and rejuvenating sleep. *Examples: cozy beds with soft pillows and blankets, or someone peacefully asleep.* These visuals emphasize the value of getting adequate rest.

Terms

- Positive affirmations: Write down empowering affirmations that uplift and motivate you. *Examples: 'I am worthy of self-care,' 'I prioritize my well-being,' or 'I am resilient and strong.'*

- Self-love and compassion: Include words that emphasize self-love and self-compassion. *Examples: 'Love yourself,' 'Be kind to yourself,' or 'Embrace self-acceptance.'*

- Balance and harmony: Choose words that convey a sense of balance and harmony in your life. *Examples: 'Balance,' 'Harmony,' or 'Equilibrium.'*

- Mindfulness and presence: Incorporate words that encourage being mindful and present in the moment. *Examples: 'Mindful,' 'Present,' or 'Breathe.'*

- Gratitude: Include words related to gratitude and appreciation. *Examples: 'Grateful,' 'Thankful,' or 'Appreciation.'*

- Wellness and health: Select words that emphasize overall health and wellness. *Examples: 'Wellness,' 'Vitality,' or 'Health.'*

- Relaxation and renewal: Use words that symbolize relaxation and rejuvenation. *Examples: 'Relax,' 'Renew,' or 'Recharge.'*

- Strength and resilience: Include words that highlight your inner strength and resilience. *Examples: 'Strength,' 'Resilience,' or 'Courage.'*

- Connection and relationships: Choose words that represent meaningful connections and nurturing relationships. *Examples: 'Connection,' 'Nurture,' or 'Bond.'*

- Joy and happiness: Incorporate words that evoke feelings of joy and happiness. *Examples: 'Joyful,' 'Happiness,' or 'Delight.'*

- Simplicity and clarity: Use words that suggest simplifying life and gaining clarity. *Examples: 'Simplify,' 'Clarity,' or 'Focus.'*

- Time for self: Emphasize the importance of setting aside time for self-care. Examples: *'Me time,' 'Self-care,' or 'Self-compassion.'*

When selecting words for your self-care vision board, choose those that resonate with your goals and intentions. These words will serve as daily reminders of your commitment to self-care practices and help you stay motivated on your journey to well-being and healing after narcissistic abuse.

Schedule some time each day for meditation

As we saw in Chapter 6, meditation is a great daily practice to calm your nervous system and start to shift back online and into presence. This can be challenging at first, but even starting with two minutes a day is beneficial.

An example of a great meditation is a 10-minute body scan. Once you've mastered the shorter body scan on page 101 with daily practice, you can move on to this longer one and really start to step into your higher self.

Ten-minute body scan meditation

This meditation encourages relaxation and mindfulness by bringing attention to different parts of the body.

- Find a quiet and comfortable place to sit or lie down. Close your eyes gently if you feel comfortable doing so, or keep them softly focused on a spot in front of you.

- Start by taking a few deep breaths, inhaling deeply through your nose, and exhaling slowly through your mouth. Let go of any tension or stress with each exhale.

- Now, bring your focus to your toes. Imagine a warm, gentle light at the tips of your toes. Feel this warm light slowly spreading, soothing, and relaxing each toe one by one.

- Move your attention up to your feet. Feel the relaxation moving through the soles of your feet, your arches, and your heels. Let go of any tension in your feet as you continue to breathe deeply.

- Now, shift your awareness to your ankles and calves. Imagine the warm light enveloping these areas, releasing any tightness or discomfort.

- Move up to your knees, thighs, and hips. With each breath, feel the tension melting away, leaving your lower body feeling light and relaxed.

- Now, focus on your lower back and abdomen. Allow the warmth to flow through these areas, relieving any stress or tightness you might be holding.

- Bring your attention to your chest and upper back. Feel the rise and fall of your breath as you inhale and exhale. Let go of any tension in your chest and upper back muscles.

- Shift your awareness to your hands and fingers. Imagine the warm light spreading to each fingertip, soothing and relaxing your hands completely.

- Move up to your wrists, forearms, and elbows. Feel the relaxation extending through these areas, allowing any lingering tension to dissolve.

- Now, bring your focus to your shoulders. Imagine them becoming lighter and free from any burdens as the warm light envelops them.

- Move up to your neck and throat. Let go of any tightness or constriction in this area, allowing your breath to flow effortlessly.

- Finally, direct your attention to your head and face. Feel the warm light gently relaxing the muscles in your jaw, cheeks, and forehead. Let go of any furrows or clenches.

- Take a few moments to experience the full relaxation of your entire body. Enjoy the sense of peace and calm that comes with this mindfulness practice.

- When you're ready, begin to slowly bring your awareness back to the room. Wiggle your fingers and toes, gently move your body, and open your eyes.

This body scan meditation is a powerful tool for relaxation and self-awareness. Regular practice can help reduce stress, improve sleep, and promote overall well-being.

Loving kindness meditation

One of my favorite meditations is the loving kindness meditation. This is a well-known meditation that is used a lot in positive psychology as it can help develop feelings of compassion and kindness to oneself first and then others.[3] The loving kindness meditation is a centuries-old Buddhist practice called 'Metta.' It has its roots in Buddhist traditions and teachings, though its precise origins cannot be traced back to a single person. The practice has been transmitted through numerous Buddhist schools and generations.

The main goal of loving kindness meditation is to cultivate and spread feelings of love and goodwill, first toward oneself and subsequently toward others, including family members, friends, and even people we may disagree or have problems with. But remember, to heal doesn't mean you need to forgive the narcissist; on the contrary, forgiveness is actually about forgiving the younger version of yourself who did not know what you now know (we'll delve into this more deeply in Chapter 11). This meditation encourages compassion, comprehension, and the removal of obstacles that exist.

Loving kindness meditation is practiced all over the world as a way to develop a heart that is full of love and compassion for the benefit of oneself and all beings. Below, you'll find the script of the loving kindness meditation. I invite you to use your phone or tablet to record yourself speaking the meditation. Try listening to it every day for 28 days, and see if you notice a difference in how you feel. I find the words in this meditation beautiful because they really speak to your self-healing with kindness and compassion.

- Begin by getting yourself comfortable. Allow yourself to switch from your usual mode of doing to non-doing, to simply being. Connect with your body and bring your attention to your breathing.

- Follow your breath as it comes in, and then out of your body, without trying to change it. Simply be aware of it, and any feelings associated with it. Give full attention to each in-breath and then to each out-breath. Be totally present and in the moment with each breath. If distracting thoughts arise, acknowledge them without becoming involved and return to the practice.

- Take a moment now to consciously set an intention for this practice. Some examples are: 'To open my heart,' 'To cultivate loving kindness,' 'To care for myself.'

- Bring to mind a person or a pet whom you are happy to see and for whom you have deep feelings of love. Imagine or sense this person or pet, noticing the feelings you have for them arise in your body. It may be a smile that spreads across your face; it may be a warmth in your body. Whatever it is, allow it to be felt.

- Let go of this person or pet, but continue to stay aware of the feelings that have arisen. Focusing on these feelings, see if you can offer loving kindness to yourself, by letting these words become your words:

    May I be safe. May I be happy. May I be healthy.
    May I live in peace, no matter what I am given.
    May my heart be filled with love and kindness.

- Notice the feelings and sensations that arise and let them be. Now try offering loving kindness to someone who supports you. Bring that person to mind and let these words become your words:

  May you be safe. May you be happy. May you be healthy.
  May you live in peace, no matter what you are given.
  May your heart be filled with love and kindness.

- Notice the feelings and sensations that arise and let them be. Once feelings for a loved one flow easily, turn your attention to someone with whom you have difficulty. It's best not to start with the most difficult person, but someone who brings up feelings of slight annoyance or irritation. See if you can let these words become your words as you keep this person in awareness:

  May you be safe. May you be happy. May you be healthy.
  May you live in peace, no matter what you are given.
  May your heart be filled with love and kindness.

- Notice the feelings and sensations that arise, and see if you can just allow them, and let them be. Now bring to mind the broader community of which you are a part. Imagine your family, your colleagues, your neighbors; fan out your attention until you include yourself in this offering of loving kindness as you let these words become your words:

  May we be safe. May we be happy. May we be healthy.
  May we live in peace, no matter what we are given.
  May our hearts be filled with love and kindness.

- Notice the sensations and feelings that arise within you. Sit with them for a few moments until you are ready to end the practice.

Write a self-compassion letter

This is a positive psychology intervention that focuses on self-acceptance and self-support.

Step 1: Reflect on your perceived inadequacy from experiencing narcissistic abuse

Begin by acknowledging an aspect of yourself or your life that you have struggled with due to the effects of narcissistic abuse. This could be something that triggers feelings of shame, unworthiness, inadequacy, or self-consciousness. It may pertain to your appearance, career, relationships, health, parenting, or any other aspect. Write down your thoughts, feelings, and emotions surrounding this perceived inadequacy. Allow yourself to delve into the depths of your emotions. What thoughts or stories emerge when you think about the narcissistic abuse you have experienced in this aspect of yourself or your life?

Step 2: Offer yourself unconditional love and acceptance

Imagine a dear friend or a compassionate mentor – one who embodies unconditional love, acceptance, and support. Visualize this friend looking at you with kindness, not only seeing your strengths, but also acknowledging the areas where you struggle. This friend forgives, accepts, and embraces you just as you are, without judgment. Now, write a letter to yourself from the perspective of this kind friend. Let your words flow with gentleness, empathy, and nonjudgmental acceptance. Express what this loving friend would say to you about the perceived inadequacy. How would they demonstrate compassion and support? How would they encourage you to take steps toward positive change? There's no need to overthink the phrasing or structure; simply write from a place of deep kindness and understanding.

Step 3: Reconnect with self-compassion

After completing the letter, set it aside for at least 15 minutes, or longer if you prefer. Allow the emotions to settle and notice the sensations in your body. If tears want to flow, let them, and just hold yourself with your right hand under your left armpit and your left hand around your arm like you are giving yourself a hug. Feel your own body in the here and now to bring you back into a place of presence. When you return to the letter, take your time to read it with an open heart. Let the words resonate deeply within you. Feel the encouragement, support, compassion, and acceptance conveyed in the letter. Allow every positive word to flow into your being.

Use this letter as a source of comfort and encouragement whenever you find yourself feeling down or struggling with self-doubt. Keep it by your bed or even in your bag. It serves as a reminder of the self-acceptance and self-support that are integral to your healing process. Recognize that providing yourself with love and understanding is the first step toward initiating positive change and reclaiming your sense of self-worth. This intervention encourages you to be your own source of comfort and support, promoting self-compassion as you navigate the path to healing from narcissistic abuse. It helps heal the codependency as it pulls you away from looking to others to heal you, instead utilizing what you already have inside of you.

Strength-Based Approaches

Positive psychology encourages you to identify and cultivate your strengths and virtues. Rather than fixating on perceived weaknesses or flaws, this approach shifts the focus toward personal growth and empowerment. Strength-based interventions help you develop a sense of competence, self-worth, and agency, all of which are essential for lifting the burden of shame. If you want to find out what your top strengths are, there are lots of free tests you can take online, for example on the VIA Institute on Character website.[4] Taking a strengths test such as this is beneficial because it helps you discover your top strengths, which can be valuable in several ways:

1. Self-awareness: It provides insight into your unique qualities and abilities, fostering self-awareness so you can bring more awareness to potentially narcissistic relationships.

2. Personal growth: Recognizing strengths can boost confidence and motivate personal growth, which can be empowering, especially after experiencing narcissistic abuse.

3. Career development: Identifying strengths can guide career choices and job satisfaction. Narcissists aren't just romantic; they can also have an impact on your career. Leaning into your strengths brings more meaning and clarity to your work and career progression.

4. Better relationships: There's always a fear after a relationship with a narcissist that you won't be able to form positive relationships, but knowing your strengths, leaning into them, and honoring them moves you towards more flourishing relationships.

5. Effective problem-solving: Utilizing strengths can lead to more effective problem-solving and decision-making. Often, we lack self-trust after a relationship with a narcissist, so using our strengths can start to rebuild the self-trust in our decision-making processes.

I've found that people who identify their strengths and are either still in an active relationship with a narcissist, or who have just come out of one, will have kindness and honesty as one of their top five. The first time I did this, honesty was my top strength, kindness was my third, and love was my last! Given that honesty was completely lacking in my marriage, no wonder I felt like I was on edge all the time and out of alignment.

Daily exceptions journal

This exercise, adapted from Fredrike Bannink's 'Exceptions Journal' exercise, helps move from what is wrong with you to what is right with you, and from what is not working to what is.[5] This exercise uses positive CBT (classic CBT integrated with positive psychology) to emphasize and explore exceptions to the problem, rather than the problem itself, with the goal of improving your well-being.

The theory behind this tool is healthy self-monitoring. You're encouraged to create an 'exceptions journal' in order to start tracking when the issue *does not* arise and why. Maybe you notice your emotional eating part not showing up as much, or you get through a weekend without crying, or you don't shout at your children.

Keeping track of when a problematic behavior *does not* occur in our day helps us to learn about what we are doing right to manage it and heal from narcissistic abuse. Over the next seven days, spend some time at the end of each day answering the following questions:

1. What has improved today, even if just a little bit?

2. What else has improved?

3. What did I do differently to improve things?

4. What did I think or believe about myself that was helpful to make these improvements? What was different?

5. When didn't I experience the problem today?

6. What happens when the problem begins to resolve itself? What am I doing to bring this resolution about?

7. When was the problem less of a problem today?

8. What could I do to continue to make improvements?

9. What would my life look like if things continued to improve?

10. What can I congratulate myself for today?

Can you start to see why positive psychology is so important to add into your healing as you start to look at your life through a different lens?

Gratitude Practice

Gratitude is a potent positive psychology intervention that can counteract feelings of shame and unworthiness. Regularly reflecting on the things we're grateful for can foster a sense of appreciation of life's blessings. This practice not only boosts mood, but also redirects attention away from negative self-perceptions. There will always be something that we can find to be grateful for and we often lose this when we're in the throes of trying to heal from narcissistic abuse.

Gratitude was something that I used to really struggle with because I was blaming everyone else for how I was feeling. What did I possibly have to be grateful for? My life was like a train wreck! But by using all the tools that I'm going to show you, I started to realize that everyone was actually doing the best they could from their programming, even the narcissist. Gratitude is part of my daily practice now – even if I've had a tough day, there will still be small things that I can sit with and be truly grateful for.

THE BENEFITS OF GRATITUDE IN YOUR HEALING JOURNEY

Gratitude is a potent tool in your multilayered healing journey after narcissistic abuse for a number of reasons:

- By encouraging an appreciation of your blessings, rather than focusing on your misfortune of narcissistic abuse, gratitude helps you see the bright side of life.

- By helping you recognize your own strengths and resources, cultivating appreciation helps increase resilience.

- Gratitude can help you process and let go of negative emotions related to your experiences of narcissistic abuse, which is an important step in the healing process. Feelings of calm and equilibrium are fostered.

- Rebuilding self-esteem after narcissistic abuse is difficult, but gratitude can help – gratitude promotes self-compassion and self-appreciation, both of which are necessary for healing and are often absent during narcissistic abuse.

- Gratitude has been shown to improve relationships, which is especially helpful when you may have endured isolation and manipulation.

- Gratitude fosters a positive outlook and a willingness to look forward, which are essential for moving past the trauma of narcissistic abuse and into a better life.

Below are some little gratitude habits that you can incorporate into your day. Practice doing some of these over the next 28 days and notice what sensations you start to feel in your body and whether you notice any shifts in your bodily sensations.

Random outreach

Reach out to someone you're thankful for, but whom you don't often tell how much you appreciate them. This could be via email, handwritten note, phone call, or text message. Describe in detail the things you appreciate about them.

Expressing thankfulness right away

Send a short email or leave a brief message after someone does something for you that you appreciate, outlining the specific action(s) they took and how it made you feel.

Greetings and appreciations

Every time you meet someone, start the conversation by expressing your gratitude for one aspect of that person. Appreciation fosters a welcoming, honest, and open atmosphere that can improve communication and strengthen the relationship.

Slow it down

During the first 10 bites of every meal, pay attention to every bite you take. Slowly chew the food, taking note of its flavor as it breaks down, and your stomach filling up with each swallow. Thank the food for keeping you healthy. As you keep doing this, you'll discover that eating more slowly causes you to feel fuller more quickly.

Evening appreciation

Establish a custom for everyone in your family to share one thing they are grateful for that day at dinner to foster a sense of community and connection among family members. I recently did this on holiday, and it was amazing to see my children find joy and gratitude in the smallest of moments.

The present and the future

Every night, write down three things you're thankful for today and three things you'll be thankful for tomorrow. Imagine that each future state of thankfulness has already occurred. Take note of how you feel as you consider each prospective action. Are you excited, happy, calm? Take whatever emotion you're feeling and hang on to it until you drift off to sleep. Notice if this improves flashbacks or promises a deeper sleep routine for you.

Triggered? Go back to being grateful

Start being aware of your triggers. People frequently become agitated in situations like being cut off in traffic, standing in a queue at the grocery store, waiting for their internet to connect, or waiting for a text to be received when their coverage is poor. Take three deep breaths and focus on something for which you are grateful whenever you feel aggravation or anger starting to rise within you. This will help you regain control of your emotions so that they don't sweep you off your feet. Bring awareness to that nervous system dysregulation as you find an alternative pathway to soothe yourself. Doing this regularly creates new neural pathways of safety and positivity.

Gratitude promotes self-compassion
and self-appreciation.

Positive Affirmations

We touched on positive affirmations earlier in the book. They're such a simple yet powerful tool to challenge your negative self-beliefs. On their own, without the work you've done on the nervous system in the previous chapter, they will have less effect, but by integrating positive affirmations with trauma work, you'll have a brilliant recipe for feeling better. By repeating positive statements about yourself, you can start to rewire your thought patterns, gradually replacing self-critical inner dialogue with self-affirming ones, such as:

- 'I am enough.'

- 'I am worthy.'

- 'I am lovable.'

- 'I am important.'

While these may speak to the classic inner child wounds, you may have another affirmation that feels more important and powerful to you. Mine have changed as I've gone along my healing journey – from 'I am enough,' to 'I am lovable,' to 'I am important,' and the ones I use now are 'I matter' and 'I belong.' Make them personal to you.

I then want you to put this affirmation everywhere. Change your passwords to reflect it, write it on Post-it notes and pop them around the house (including one right by the bed so you see it the moment you wake up), put it in lipstick or eye liner on your bathroom mirrors so that, as you clean your teeth, you see your personal positive affirmation. This repetition, with nervous system regulation, can really start to shift that negative self-talk and calm the inner critic protector response as you start to feel more present, not stuck in the past.

This transformative journey is not a linear path, but a dynamic process that unfolds over time. It involves setbacks and challenges, but with resilience and self-compassion as companions, you can become better equipped to face adversity and overcome obstacles, even after the narcissist. The integration of positive psychology interventions with nervous system regulation offers a powerful combination to lift the weight of shame and build strength and resilience, equipping you with the tools to thrive, even during life's inevitable trials. This harmonious approach empowers you to not only heal, but also flourish. That may seem a paradox – that you can heal and thrive in the face of abuse – but it is possible when we work on the symptoms and root cause.

By addressing the physiological and psychological aspects of shame, you can lift the burden of self-criticism, nurture your self-worth, and build resilience. This integrative approach empowers you to flourish as you rediscover your inner strength and capacity for happiness and fulfillment, because it's all possible and it's all available to you.

In this chapter, you have learned lots of interventions and exercises, and I encourage you to try all of them. Notice how you start to feel as the possibilities of a life filled with joy, connection, and meaning start to emerge. As you continue, you'll start to feel real shifts as we heal the past for a better future.

What if narcissistic abuse could actually be the biggest wake-up call you've ever had? What if you can go on and lead an amazing life *because* of this trauma from the narcissist? I hope you're starting to see why experiencing narcissistic abuse can really open your eyes to what you have experienced and how you can take back your power. You're here reading this, right now, and you wouldn't be had you not experienced narcissistic abuse.

Part III of this book will support you in stepping into your best self with compassion and an understanding of your past – even if it's just teeny tiny steps to start with. A tiny step is still better than no step at all and you're here, so celebrate that step. These later chapters may be challenging initially for you as they're going against the perception of what we feel we should be experiencing. But finding a sense of meaning in the trauma of narcissistic abuse doesn't take away what you have been through and experienced.

PART III

Stepping into
Your Best Self

CHAPTER 8

Finding Meaning and Purpose in Narcissistic Abuse

I know you may read the title of this chapter and think... 'WHAT?! How can you ever find meaning and purpose from being abused by a narcissist?' As we move through this chapter together, I entreat you to put your skepticism to one side and hold an openness and curiosity to the possibilities of leading an even better life because of your experience of narcissistic abuse.

In this chapter, we'll look at turning your pain and struggle into your biggest strength and purpose. We're going to explore a positive psychology framework called the PERMAH profile, which gives you six key pillars to focus on so that you can continue to deepen your healing and well-being. By focusing on these six pillars, you can, from an evidence-based perspective, start to feel happier. It is possible, because I am living proof. Wherever you are on your journey to heal and thrive, hold this thought, and open yourself up to the idea that maybe, just maybe, this a possibility for you too.

SELF-COMPASSION AS A FOUNDATION

Central to the journey of turning pain into purpose is self-compassion. You need to learn to treat yourself with the same kindness, understanding, and love that you would offer a friend. Self-compassion involves embracing imperfections, forgiving yourself for perceived shortcomings, and fostering a sense of inner warmth and acceptance. We'll talk more about forgiveness in the final chapter as it's such an important part of the healing process (though it's not about needing to forgive the narcissist).

Self-compassion allows you to soothe your emotional wounds and build resilience. It serves as a foundation upon which the process of transformation can unfold. If you feel you need to do more work here, please revisit Chapter 7 and engage in the self-compassion tools outlined there.

The PERMAH Profile: A Path to Healing After Narcissistic Abuse

Positive psychology focuses on human flourishing, well-being, and the factors that contribute to a fulfilling life. One of the key frameworks within positive psychology is the PERMAH model, which outlines six essential elements for lasting happiness and well-being. Understanding and implementing the PERMAH profile when healing from narcissistic abuse can be a powerful tool for healing and personal growth.

The PERMAH model, introduced by Martin Seligman in his book *Flourish*, serves as a foundational framework within positive psychology and is an incredible tool for you to utilize in your healing transformation.[1] It initially identified five key elements that contribute to a flourishing and fulfilling life, but then studies revealed this was only a neck-up approach and the H was then added:

- **Positive Emotions (P):** This element focuses on experiencing good feelings such as joy, gratitude, love, and contentment. Positive emotions serve as a buffer against negative emotions and contribute to overall well-being.

- **Engagement (E):** Engagement refers to the state of 'flow' or being fully absorbed and immersed in an activity. When individuals are engaged in their pursuits, they often lose track of time and experience a sense of fulfillment.

- **Relationships (R):** Human beings are inherently social creatures, and positive relationships with others play a vital role in well-being. Nurturing meaningful connections with family, friends, and community members fosters a sense of belonging and support.

- **Meaning (M):** Meaning involves having a sense of purpose in life and feeling that one's actions contribute to something greater than ourselves. It encompasses values, goals, and a sense of direction.

- **Accomplishment (A):** Accomplishment pertains to setting and achieving goals that are personally meaningful. The pursuit of mastery and achievement leads to a sense of competence and satisfaction.

- **Health (H):** Health looks at the three key aspects of sleep, nutrition, and exercise, although I like to use the word 'movement' from a trauma-informed perspective as I know that 'exercise' can conjure up self-doubt and fears of not wanting to be seen at a gym.

By cultivating positive emotions, engagement, positive relationships, meaning, accomplishment, and health, you can reclaim your sense of self-worth and rebuild your life.

The development of the PERMAH profile means that you can track – from a real-time, evidence-based standpoint – what you need to work on the most in your life from the six pillars to start to increase your well-being.

The PERMAH profile questionnaire assesses various aspects of well-being and happiness based on Martin Seligman's PERMAH theory.[2] Below is the questionnaire for you to complete.

PERMAH PROFILE
QUESTIONNAIRE

Please rate the following statements on a scale from 1 to 5, with 1 being 'strongly disagree' and 5 being 'strongly agree.'

Positive Emotions (P)

- I generally feel optimistic about the future.

- I often experience joy and happiness in my daily life.

- I find it easy to maintain a positive outlook, even in challenging situations.

- I frequently express gratitude for the good things in my life.

- I am generally content and satisfied with my life.

Engagement (E)

- I often lose track of time when I'm engrossed in an enjoyable activity.

- I feel a sense of flow and focus in my work or hobbies.

- I actively seek out new challenges and experiences to engage with.

- I'm highly motivated and energized by my daily tasks.

- I'm fully immersed in the present moment in various aspects of my life.

Relationships (R)

- I have strong and supportive relationships with family and friends.

- I feel a deep sense of connection and belonging in my social circles.

- I regularly invest time and effort in nurturing my relationships.

- I'm a good listener and communicate effectively with others.

- I can rely on my relationships for emotional support and companionship.

Meaning (M)

- I feel that my life has a sense of purpose and direction.

- I find fulfillment in contributing to causes or activities I care about.

- I often reflect on the deeper meaning and significance of my experiences.

- I believe that my actions and choices align with my values and beliefs.

- I derive a sense of meaning from my daily life and responsibilities.

Accomplishment (A)

- I frequently set and achieve meaningful goals in various areas of my life.

- I take pride in my accomplishments and personal growth.

- I'm highly motivated to pursue success in my endeavors.

- I handle setbacks and failures with resilience and determination.

- I feel a strong sense of achievement and satisfaction.

Health (H)

- I prioritize and maintain a healthy lifestyle through diet and movement.

- I regularly engage in activities that promote my physical and mental well-being.

- I manage stress effectively and practice relaxation techniques.

- I get enough restful sleep to feel energized and refreshed.

- I take proactive steps to address my overall health and well-being.

After completing the questionnaire, tally your scores for each category to gain insight into your well-being and happiness in different areas of life. The higher your score, the better. Look for areas where your score is lower – these are the key areas to start to work on first. I would suggest initially choosing two and working on them, and then the next two, and so on. I do my own personal PERMAH profile every six months, even now, to give myself a personal check-in to ensure I am always working on my well-being and not just processing the past.

The PERMAH model can give you a blueprint to focus on how to live a more thriving and flourishing life after narcissistic abuse. I print off my PERMAH profile and stick it on my fridge so I don't get sidetracked focusing on things that won't make a difference to my well-being.

Let's now dive deeper into the PERMAH model and explore how you can use it as a daily framework to heal, survive, and thrive after narcissistic abuse.

Positive Emotions (P) in Narcissistic Abuse Healing

Narcissistic abuse often leaves you with a barrage of negative emotions, including anger, sadness, guilt, and shame. These can be overwhelming and debilitating. However, the first element of the PERMAH model – positive emotions – can serve as a valuable counterbalance to these negative feelings.

In the context of healing after narcissistic abuse, fostering positive emotions involves engaging in activities and practices that bring joy and contentment. This might include reconnecting with hobbies and interests that were abandoned during the abusive relationship, spending time with supportive friends and family, and engaging in self-care routines that promote relaxation and well-being.

Positive emotions not only provide relief from the emotional pain, but also create a foundation of resilience and hope. They remind you that joy and happiness are still attainable and worth pursuing.

The three states of mind

When we're experiencing narcissistic abuse, one second we can be completely sensible and calm, and the next we can be an emotional mess. Maybe you've had conversations with friends or partners that seemed sensible, only to find yourself in a screaming rage 20 minutes later with no idea how you got there. This demonstrates how quickly we can shift from logical to emotional mental states – online to offline (see page 113). Just like we've discussed in previous chapters, depending on what our nervous system perceives, we'll be up and down those Traffic Lights of Tolerance™! The logical mind, the emotional mind, and the wise mind are the three diverse mental states that we might experience.

Logical mind

When thinking rationally, in the neocortex, you approach problems intellectually, planning and choosing mostly based on logic and facts rather than emotions or values. You are subject to the laws of logic, reason, and fact in this mode. Making a shopping list, devising a recipe from scratch, and planning a train route to a new location are examples of exercising a logical mind.

Being rational can be advantageous. Without it, we would be unable to construct buildings, roads, or cities; follow directions; solve logical puzzles; conduct scientific research; or conduct meetings. However, if you place too much emphasis on the logical mind, your life and decisions will become nearly 'computer-like,' 'robotic,' with little room for your unique needs, intuition, and spontaneity, and understanding that you're a human with emotions and past traumatic experiences. Just try to imagine yourself making a rational decision to purchase a new home without taking into account questions like, 'Do I feel at home in this house?' or 'Can I see myself living happily in this house?' You would base your decision to purchase the home only on the available information, such as, 'Will this house be a good investment?' or 'Is this house in good condition?'

Emotional mind

In the emotional mind, the limbic system, all of your decisions are made based only on how you're feeling at the time, which is grounded in your interpretation from your past experiences. This means that experiencing narcissistic abuse can bring about huge surges in emotion – then factor in your childhood, and you can see why emotions override logic. When your emotions direct and affect your thoughts and actions, you're in the emotional mind. Facts, logic, and reason go completely out of the window. Examples of the emotional mind include hastily hurting a loved one's feelings or immediately singing along to the radio when your favorite song comes on.

The emotional mind has many uses. You can persevere in challenging work with intense devotion or drive, and you can improve relationships with others by impulsively complimenting them while you're feeling upbeat. However, issues with the emotional mind arise when a behavior brought on by an emotion, such as the hurt from the narcissist, has immediate or long-lasting detrimental effects. For instance, feeling happy might make you do something unsafe, while being angry might make you hurt someone, even yourself. Going back to the house-buying example above, operating from an emotional place could result in purchasing a home with many defects and unpleasant surprises.

Wise mind

There is a middle ground to the logical and emotional mind: the wise mind. We can concurrently listen to our hearts and heads in a wise mind, depending on the circumstance. We recognize the worth of both reason and emotion in this mentality. We may relate to our emotions without letting them consume us, as we need to validate ourselves in why we may feel like that. We pay attention to the voice of reason while maintaining our connection to our feelings and core convictions. Knowing through observation, knowing through logical analysis, knowing through what we experience in our nervous system, knowing through what we do, and knowing through intuition are all integrated in the wise mind. For instance, acting with wisdom would entail taking into account both the facts and your feelings when deciding whether to purchase a new home – there's a balance.

Trauma healing helps us step into the wise mind more frequently.

WISE MIND CHAIR EXERCISE

The Wise Mind Chair is one of my all-time favorite positive psychology exercises, and I use it a lot with my clients and in groups. It really helps you honor and validate, with kindness and compassion, that you have emotions, but that there is also logic and rationality to any situation. The Wise Mind Chair is about making decisions, but in the positive self state.

Picture three chairs in front of you. The first chair represents your logical mind, the second chair represents your emotional mind, and the third chair represents your wise mind. Your task is to adopt each mental state symbolized by the appropriate chair while I pose a series of questions to you. The goal is to familiarize yourself with the many mental states you employ on a daily basis and how to navigate these with compassion and kindness to yourself, and to help you make decisions not only based on emotion, but also on logic and rationality.

Step 1: Pick a circumstance

Pick a circumstance or recollection with the narcissist that you find difficult. This could be to do with the children, maybe your parents, or even going through court. For a brief period, close your eyes and give the scenario as much room as possible to develop in your thoughts.

Step 2: Use your best judgment

The rational and logical mind chair is available for your use. Answer these questions to give you an idea of what it's like to approach this challenging circumstance with a logical mind:

- What are the 'hard' truths of this circumstance?

- What would be the most logical answer in light of the available factual evidence?

- What proof do I have for my position?

- How would I resolve this issue?

- No matter what 'right' feels like, what is the best course of action?

Step 3: Use your emotional mind

Next, shift into the emotional mind chair. Answer these questions from the emotional mind chair about the circumstance with the narcissist to give you an idea of what it's like to approach this challenging circumstance with your emotional mind.

- What feelings do I have about this circumstance?

- How noxious is the feeling?

- How strong is the feeling?

- Whatever happens, what do I feel like doing right now?

- What, regardless of the repercussions, do I feel like expressing at this moment?

Step 4: Develop a wise mindset

Now, sit in the wise mind chair. First, focus on the present moment. Spend a minute or so concentrating on your breath, attempting to maintain awareness of your breath throughout. Now apply the wise mind to this challenging scenario with the narcissist and answer these questions:

- What do my feelings tell me about what I most need right now?

- How can I weigh the evidence while attending to my needs right now?

- What does the larger context resemble?

- What does my gut feeling say about this circumstance?

- Which of my qualities or talents could I apply to this situation?

- What can I take away from this experience?

- How can I react to the circumstance in a way that reflects the kind of person I hope to become?

Step 5: Assessment

Reflect on the steps above and consider the following questions:

- Do you ever find yourself applying your rational and logical mind when your wise mind may be more appropriate?

- Do you ever find yourself using your emotional mind when your wise mind may be more appropriate?

- What advantages might you gain from spending more time in the wise mind?

- What advantages would accrue to those around you if you spent more time in the wise mind?

Can you start to see that often we sit only in the emotional mind? We don't want to invalidate and eradicate what has happened to us, because our nervous system is trying to build capacity as we heal, but we want to try to make as good decisions as we can for ourselves and not base them purely on emotion. I know this can be very hard when healing after narcissistic abuse as everything feels so heightened.

You can use the Wise Mind Chair exercise for any big decision you need to make, to help honor your emotions but make better choices for yourself.

Engagement (E) as a Path to Recovery

Engagement, or the state of 'flow,' is another essential component of the PERMAH model that can greatly aid in the healing process after narcissistic abuse. When you're engaged in activities that captivate your attention and challenge your skills, you experience a sense of fulfillment and distraction from emotional distress.

In the aftermath of narcissistic abuse, you may have lost touch with activities you once loved or felt passionate about. I used to love sport and listening to music, and I completely stopped doing these when I was with my ex-husband. Rediscovering these pursuits can be an empowering step in your healing journey.

Whether it's art, music, sports, or any other hobby, engagement in these activities can help you regain a sense of purpose and self-identity.

Engagement also extends to the process of self-reflection and personal growth. You can engage in self-help practices that allow you to explore your emotions, thoughts, and beliefs. This introspective engagement can lead to greater self-awareness and a clearer sense of your values and goals.

Start to think of as many flow-producing activities as you can and write them down. You should keep in mind that flow activities are those in which you feel totally absorbed and engaged, so much so that you lose track of time and self-consciousness. Writing this book is a flow experience for me. Examples can be things like skiing, gardening, cooking, reading, knitting, and visiting friends. Start to think about what activities you're most drawn to. For flow to occur, three conditions must be met: clarity of a goal, immediate feedback on progress, and balanced skill level versus challenge being faced. So, think what activities you have chosen that could meet these criteria. For example, writing this book is a goal, I get immediate feedback as I send in my chapters to my editor, and this is a skill but also a challenge as it can feel scary!

Flow is a state we often don't find ourselves in when healing as we're often dissociated, which is the complete opposite of flow. For flow to occur, we need to find an activity that fits this criterion and keep working on our nervous system regulation so we can stay focused on the activity. What would your flow activity be to work on the E in your PERMAH profile?

Relationships (R) and Healing

Positive relationships, a fundamental element of the PERMAH model, are pivotal in the healing process after narcissistic abuse because some of us may have never experienced a healthy relationship. A common tactic used by narcissists to isolate you is to sever your ties with supportive friends and family members. Consequently, you may find yourself feeling profoundly alone and disconnected. I know I certainly did. I felt no one understood and, over the years, I completely isolated myself other than from the children's activities.

Reconnecting with people after coming out of an abusive relationship with a narcissist can be a crucial step in your healing process as people may not have known about, or realized, the extent of the trauma you have experienced. They may still not know, but that's OK because you know and that's enough. It's essential to approach this process with care and patience. Firstly, start by reaching out to a trusted friend or family member whom you feel comfortable talking to and maybe have isolated yourself from. Share your experiences and feelings at your own pace, allowing them to provide support and understanding. You can say something like, 'I've been through a difficult time, and I'd appreciate someone to talk to and reconnect with.' Maybe apologize that you haven't contacted them as this shows ownership, with the hope this will be met with compassion and kindness.

Seeking support from trustworthy friends and family members who can provide emotional validation and understanding, not keep you trapped in drama-filled conversations, offers a sense of belonging and safety, countering the isolation imposed by the narcissist.

Additionally, you can benefit from joining support groups like my free Facebook group (*see Resources, page 239*), where there's a great sense of community with others who have endured similar experiences, fostering empathy and shared healing.

YOU CAN'T CO-PARENT WITH A NARCISSIST

Society has a lot to answer for, as you're deemed a bad parent if you're unable to co-parent effectively with your ex. This is when society doesn't understand narcissistic abuse. I believe that the starting point where abuse has been present should instead be 'parallel parenting.'

Parallel parenting:

- places the focus on the child instead of the parents
- protects the child's relationship with both parents
- increases the child's chances for success
- reduces conflict between the parents
- reduces the amount of time spent in court

Parallel parenting can be compared to train tracks: The rails of a train track run consistently side by side, never touching, yet still effectively helping to move the train from one place to another. Similarly, two people can parent in a parallel fashion, never communicating directly, yet still successfully raising their child mutually.

How parallel parenting works

- Parents disengage and have little to no interaction with each other. In the event of emergencies, parents will communicate.

- The schedule is documented in detail and placed on a calendar. Nothing is left to interpretation because loopholes breed conflict.

- Each parent's household functions independently; each parent is responsible for making decisions about the child during the time that the child is in that parent's household. *Do not tell the other parent how to parent.*

- Rather than being discussed, major decisions are communicated by the parent who has the authority to make the decision (for example, health, education, and welfare issues concerning the child).

- When parents do need to share information with each other, they will use email (ideally a whole separate email is set up purely for communication with the narcissist), a parenting notebook, a pre-appointed third party, or an online tool (never the child). Parents will avoid face-to-face communication whenever possible.

- Handovers take place at school, childcare, or during activities that minimize parental conflict.

- If any deviation or change from the agreed-upon plan or order is requested, they shall be denied. Flexibility with a narcissist will lead to further abuse. If the narcissist wants to change a plan, they must apply back to court as everything needs to be official.

Remember: You can be an AMAZING parent to your children without attempting to co-parent.

Meaning (M) as a Beacon of Hope

The concept of meaning in the PERMAH model aligns with the pursuit of purpose and a sense that one's life has significance. Narcissistic abuse can profoundly disrupt your sense of purpose and identity. You often question your worth and the meaning of your experiences. To find meaning in the aftermath of narcissistic abuse, you can embark on a journey of self-discovery and personal growth. This may involve exploring your values, passions, and goals.

Furthermore, some of you may find meaning in your healing process by becoming advocates or educators in the field of narcissistic abuse and even enroll in my Accredited Narcissistic Trauma-Informed Coaching Certification (*see Resources, page 239*). Sharing your stories and knowledge can provide a sense of purpose and a mission to prevent others from suffering similar traumas.

A good way of looking at what impact you want to have on the world is to sit and write out your eulogy. Now, I know this may seem morbid, but it will really get you thinking about what you want to do with your life and how you want to be remembered. It's a super powerful positive psychology exercise as it helps to tap into the meaning and values that you want to create in your life that you can now start to step into as you heal and thrive after narcissistic abuse.

WRITING YOUR EULOGY

Writing your eulogy is a powerful way to reflect on your life's purpose. How do you want to be remembered? What is your legacy? To engage in this exercise:

1. Set the stage: Find a quiet and comfortable place where you can focus without distractions. Have a notebook, journal, and pen, or a digital device to hand, ready to jot down your thoughts.

2. Imagine the end: Close your eyes and imagine attending your own funeral. Picture the people who would be there and the atmosphere in the room. Visualize the eulogy being delivered, highlighting the positive impact you've had on others' lives.

3. Reflect on your legacy: Start writing your eulogy as if someone else is speaking it at your funeral. Describe the person you aspire to be and the contributions you hope to have made to the world. Reflect on the values, achievements, and qualities you want to be remembered for.

4. Consider the impact: Think about the people you've touched, the changes you've inspired, and the difference you've made. Include specific stories or examples of your impact on individuals, communities, or causes.

5. Explore your relationships: Look at the relationships and experiences that have enriched your life. Acknowledge those who have supported and influenced you along the way.

6. Revise and reflect: Review what you've written and make any necessary revisions. Reflect on the emotions and insights that arose during this exercise.

7. Set intentions: Use this exercise as an opportunity to set intentions for your future actions. Determine how you can align your daily choices with the legacy you want to leave.

Writing your eulogy can be a profound and motivating experience. It allows you to clarify your values, set meaningful goals, and focus on the impact you wish to have on the world.

Narcissistic abuse is a reminder to live with purpose and make choices that align with your vision of leaving a positive and lasting legacy.

> *Don't let narcissistic abuse define you —*
> *trauma need not be a lifelong sentence.*

Turning pain into purpose through advocacy

One profound way survivors can turn their pain into purpose is by becoming advocates for change. This was a massive part of my own healing journey as I became adamant about never wanting anyone else to suffer like I did for a second longer than they had to. This is why I created healing programs and teach the world's only trauma-informed coaching qualification that specializes in narcissism. I started wanting to help others heal, and then it also moved into helping others help others heal. I wanted and needed to create change and a ripple effect so we can redefine and reenvision narcissism, as it is sadly so prevalent. Many of us choose to share our stories, raising awareness about narcissistic abuse and its devastating effects. By doing so, we not only find healing, but also empower others to seek help and support. If you feel alone right now, my free Facebook support group (*see Resources, page 239*) is a great place to start. Never be alone in this, as we heal together.

Accomplishment (A) and Self-Empowerment

Accomplishment or achievement focuses on setting and achieving meaningful goals. For survivors of narcissistic abuse, setting and achieving even small goals can be a significant source of empowerment, as we have forgotten how to even do that. Small steps can lead to giant leaps, so don't try to run too fast here or your nervous system will just shut down again.

The journey of healing often involves a series of milestones and accomplishments. These might include setting boundaries with toxic individuals, not just the narcissist but others who cause drama and negativity in your life (if you want to revisit my tips on establishing boundaries, see *page 93*), rediscovering personal interests, or pursuing educational and career goals. Each achievement reinforces your sense of competence and control over your life. Moreover, accomplishing goals can be a source of pride and self-esteem. It serves as a reminder that you possess the resilience and strength to overcome adversity and create a brighter future.

Setting achievable goals

Setting achievable goals, even tiny ones, is an excellent way to make progress without feeling overwhelmed. Here are my top tips on how to do this:

1. Identify your priorities: Begin by identifying your top priorities or areas of your life where you want to make positive changes. This could be in your career, relationships, health, or personal development.

2. Break it down: Take one priority at a time and break it down into smaller, manageable parts. For example, if your priority is improving your health, you can break it down into movement, nutrition, and sleep.

3. Set specific goals: Make each part specific and measurable. Instead of a vague goal like 'Get fit,' set a specific goal like 'Walk for 20 minutes every day' or 'Eat a serving of vegetables with every meal.'

4. Start small: Begin with tiny goals that you know you can achieve. These goals should be so small that they feel easy and manageable. For example, if you want to start introducing movement into your day, your tiny goal might be to do five minutes of stretching in the morning.

5. Create a time line: Assign a time frame to each goal. Decide when you want to accomplish it. This adds a sense of urgency and accountability.

6. Write it down: Document your goals in a notebook, journal, or digital app. Writing them down makes them more concrete and helps you track your progress.

7. Take action: Start working on your tiny goals immediately. Focus on completing one goal at a time. Celebrate your achievements, no matter how small they may seem.

8. Evaluate and adjust: Regularly review your progress and adjust your goals as needed. If a tiny goal becomes too easy, make it slightly more challenging. If it feels overwhelming, make it even smaller.

9. Stay consistent: Consistency is key. Make your tiny goals a part of your daily or weekly routine. Over time, they will accumulate and lead to significant improvements.

10. Build momentum: As you achieve your tiny goals, you'll gain more confidence. This will motivate you to tackle more significant goals.

Remember that progress is a journey, and taking small, consistent steps is often more effective than trying to make significant changes all at once. Be kind to yourself. By setting and achieving tiny goals, you can gradually transform your life and avoid feeling overwhelmed.

Health (H)

While the original PERMA model primarily focused on psychological well-being, the addition of 'Health' recognizes the intricate connection between mental and physical health. This component highlights the fundamental role that maintaining good physical health plays in contributing to overall happiness and life satisfaction, and it's such an integral part of your healing after narcissistic abuse.

A robust state of health provides the necessary foundation upon which you can start to heal at a deeper, nervous system level. Without good health, it becomes challenging to fully enjoy life's pleasures, engage in fulfilling activities, foster positive relationships, pursue meaningful goals, or experience lasting happiness. We can sabotage our own healing if we ignore this aspect. My divorce diet was a glass (often a bottle) of white wine with some chili rice cakes and a tub of cheese and chive dip. The alcohol disrupted my sleep and the food was not exactly nutritiously sound. I wasn't helping myself to heal; in fact, I was slowing down my healing process.

Achieving and maintaining good health involves various factors, including regular movement, a balanced diet, sufficient sleep, stress management, and preventive healthcare practices. Physical fitness not only contributes to better health, but also enhances mood and cognitive function, promoting positive emotions and engagement. Adequate sleep is crucial for emotional regulation and mental clarity, while stress management techniques, such as mindfulness and relaxation, can significantly reduce the negative impact of chronic stress on mental and physical well-being.

'Health' underscores the necessity of holistic well-being, where physical health plays an integral role in fostering happiness and fulfillment in every aspect of life. Without our health, we have nothing. Many of you may be suffering with chronic illness – get curious about this… Is it purely physical or could your chronic illness be related to your experience of trauma and narcissistic abuse?

By following the guidelines below, you can focus on better sleep, nutrition, and movement, ultimately promoting your overall health and well-being. Remember that consistency and gradual improvements are key to long-term success. Don't beat yourself up if you have a bad day. Just try not to let it slip into a bad week or month.

Better sleep

- Establish a sleep schedule: Go to bed and wake up at the same time every day, even on weekends. This helps regulate your body's internal clock.

- Create a bedtime routine: Wind down before sleep with calming activities like reading, gentle stretches, or a warm bath. Avoid stimulating activities like watching TV or using screens.

- Create a sleep-friendly environment: Make your bedroom comfortable and conducive to sleep. Keep it dark, quiet, and cool. Invest in a comfortable mattress and pillows.

- Limit caffeine and alcohol: Avoid caffeine and alcohol close to bedtime, as they can disrupt sleep patterns.

- Stay active: Regular movement can promote better sleep, but avoid intense workouts close to bedtime.

- Manage stress: Practice relaxation techniques such as deep breathing, meditation, or progressive muscle relaxation (*see below*) to ease stress and anxiety that can interfere with sleep.

PROGRESSIVE MUSCLE RELAXATION

Here's a simple progressive muscle relaxation exercise you can try:

- Find a quiet and comfortable place to sit or lie down. Close your eyes if you like.

- Start by taking a deep breath in and then exhale slowly.

- Now, focus on your toes. Curl them up tightly for a few seconds, and then relax. Feel the tension melting away.

- Move up to your calf muscles. Tighten them for a moment, and then release. Let go of any stress.

- Next, move to your thighs. Tense them up together, and then let them go completely relaxed.

- Now, focus on your stomach. Squeeze your abdominal muscles gently, hold the tension for a moment, and then release.

- Shift your attention to your shoulders. Raise them up toward your ears, and then let them drop down, feeling the tension flow away.

- Moving to your arms, clench your fists tightly, and then release, feeling your hands become loose.

- Finally, scrunch up your face for a moment, and then let it go, allowing your facial muscles to relax.

- Take a few deep breaths, feeling the calmness spreading throughout your body.

This progressive muscle relaxation exercise is a simple way to release tension and feel more relaxed.

Nutrition

- Balanced diet: Aim for a balanced diet that includes a variety of fruits, vegetables, lean proteins, whole grains, and healthy fats.

- Regular meals: Eat regular meals and snacks throughout the day to maintain steady energy levels and avoid overeating later in the evening.

- Hydration: Stay hydrated by drinking plenty of water throughout the day. Limit sugary drinks and excessive caffeine.

- Mindful eating: Pay attention to your body's hunger and fullness cues. Avoid distracted eating in front of screens.

- Portion control: Be mindful of portion sizes to avoid overeating. Use smaller plates and bowls.

- Limit processed foods: Minimize the intake of highly processed foods, sugary snacks, and fast food. Focus on whole, unprocessed foods.

Movement

- Find enjoyable activities: Choose physical activities that you enjoy, whether that's dancing, walking, swimming, or a sport. This makes it easier to stay consistent.

- Set realistic goals: Start with achievable fitness goals. For example, aim to walk for 20 minutes a day if you're just starting out.

- Incorporate strength training: Include strength-training exercises to build muscle and support your metabolism.

- Consistency: Establish a regular routine. Aim for at least 150 minutes of moderate-intensity aerobic activity or 75 minutes of vigorous-intensity activity per week.

- Warm up and cool down: Always warm up before exercising and cool down afterward to prevent injuries.

- Listen to your body: Pay attention to your body's signals. Rest when needed and don't push through pain or discomfort.

- Consult a professional: If you have health concerns or specific fitness goals, consult a healthcare provider or a certified fitness trainer for personalized guidance.

You have now learned a tried-and-tested framework that you can consistently use to turn your pain into purpose and your struggle into strength. I recommend checking in on your profile every three to six months so that you can see which pillars you need to work on the most.

*Don't forget this part of the healing
process — you deserve to live an amazing
life. It isn't just for a select few people.*

As you progress on your healing journey, you'll discover a profound sense of personal growth and resilience. It's time to stop abandoning yourself and step into the possibilities of post-traumatic growth.

CHAPTER 9

Awakening to Post-Traumatic Growth

As you know, narcissistic abuse can leave deep emotional scars, shattering your self-esteem, trust, and overall well-being. Although recovering from such trauma is difficult, there's a powerful potential for transformation that offers hope and light at the end of what can often feel like a long, dark tunnel. In this chapter, I want to introduce you to something I'd never even heard of before I experienced narcissistic abuse, and if you'd told me about it at the height of my healing, I may have punched you! Many survivors of narcissistic abuse find a way to use their healing journey as a catalyst for personal growth and positive change — positive psychology calls this 'post-traumatic growth.'

In this chapter, we'll explore what post-traumatic growth is and how it pertains to recovering from narcissistic abuse. We'll also look at the effects post-traumatic growth can have on the remainder of your life. I hope that you'll stay on this journey with me until the end because I believe when you understand the power of post-traumatic growth, it can truly transform your life to a level you may well not have ever thought existed.

What Is Post-Traumatic Growth?

Post-traumatic growth was first introduced by psychologists Richard Tedeschi and Lawrence Calhoun in the mid-1990s. It emphasizes that trauma can be a catalyst for profound personal transformations. I see my experience of narcissistic abuse like an alarm clock. For me, my ex-husband woke me up from the freeze I'd been living my life in and made me look at my childhood with a great big spotlight. It was hard, but it was so worth it — now I don't just exist; I feel alive.

To find common patterns and aspects of post-traumatic growth, Tedeschi and Calhoun undertook a thorough body of research, including surveys and interviews with trauma survivors. They determined five key areas of growth.[1] I've outlined these below in the context of recovering from narcissistic abuse:

1. New perspectives

Narcissistic abuse can shatter our existing worldviews and beliefs. As we rebuild, we often develop a deeper understanding of life's complexities. We begin to question our values, priorities, and assumptions, leading to a more open-minded and accepting attitude toward others and ourselves. This may feel like an impossibility, but keep reading because I want to give you hope that it is possible.

2. Personal strength

Adversity forces us to tap into our inner reservoirs of resilience and strength. People who experience post-traumatic growth often discover newfound courage, determination, and the ability to cope with adversity. We often look at where we think we should be, but I encourage you to pause right here and look at how far you've come, at what you're overcoming right now. You're the one doing this, no one else. I know it can be so hard, but remember that you can do this and celebrate how far you have come.

3. Enhanced relationships

Narcissistic abuse can bring people closer together, fostering empathy, compassion, and a heightened appreciation for the support of loved ones. It strengthens our social bonds, creating a sense of belonging and interconnectedness. Reassessing current relationships and setting more sensible limits are frequently part of the healing process. Many of you may go on what I call a 'friends cleanse' as you start to see people very differently during your healing process. Some you may want to deepen your connection with, while others you may want to sever ties with. I soon realized on my healing journey that my best friend was also a covert narcissist and took great joy in my train wreck of a life, which served a purpose for her. You can gain stronger interpersonal relationships, more developed empathy, and better communication skills. In other words, you start to step into a higher version of yourself.

4. Greater meaning

Surviving narcissistic abuse often prompts a search for deeper meaning in life. Individuals may reevaluate their goals and aspirations, finding a renewed sense of purpose and direction. This can lead to a commitment to personal growth and a desire to make a positive impact on the world. This is why you're here, reading this book – you're already experiencing some post-traumatic growth, even if it's tiny right now.

5. Spiritual growth

Many people who experience post-traumatic growth report a deepening of their spiritual or existential beliefs. They may find solace and inspiration in their faith or a sense of connection to something greater than themselves. I know I definitely feel a deeper connection to myself now, as I'm more kind and caring to myself.

Post-traumatic growth covers a range of personal development areas, such as discovering new strengths, improving relationships, and developing a greater appreciation for life. It recognizes that development and trauma can coexist, giving those who have experienced trauma a path to resilience and recovery, not just now but in the future.

It's crucial to remember, though, that post-traumatic growth doesn't take away from the discomfort or suffering incurred from narcissistic abuse. It is in no way minimizing what you went through, and your experiences of narcissistic abuse. Instead, it recognizes that adversity, growth, and transformation are not incompatible with one another. The concept of post-traumatic growth offers hope and reminds us that, even in the aftermath of narcissistic abuse, there is potential for positive change and growth.

Embrace the light and hope
of what your life can be.

The road to recovery from narcissistic abuse is one-of-a-kind and intensely personal, frequently characterized by emotional upheaval, self-doubt, and damaged self-esteem. Numerous psychological and emotional issues, such as melancholy, anxiety, C-PTSD, and a pervasive sense of helplessness, can affect you as a narcissistic abuse survivor. In this situation, post-traumatic growth provides you with a ray of hope by stating that the rehabilitation process may result in growth and transformation.

It's important to understand, though, that post-traumatic growth is not a linear process and may not happen for all narcissistic abuse survivors. Because recovery is extremely individualized, you may move through different stages at your own time. You may go through spiritual or existential growth, discovering new meaning and purpose in your life. Investigating identity and personal values may be part of this. Furthermore, the path to recovery frequently includes obstacles and setbacks, and post-traumatic growth may not be immediately obvious in the short term. However, there's still room for development and transformation, which provides a glimmer of hope for you on your road to recovery, and the fact that you're reading and doing the work from this book puts you ahead of the game.

Interestingly, once you have experienced post-traumatic growth, it's unlikely to happen again. The reason for this is because on your journey of healing after narcissistic abuse or any trauma, you're building your resilience and nervous system regulation, which means that you're far better equipped to deal with any subsequent life events.

The Post-Traumatic Growth Indicator (PTGI)

Now, I'm aware that you may be reading this and thinking that you haven't experienced any post-traumatic growth and you never will, but there's a psychological tool that we can use to assess how much, however little, post-traumatic growth we have experienced.

The Post-Traumatic Growth Indicator (PTGI) is intended to quantify the positive psychological changes that can take place in people after experiencing trauma and, in our case, narcissistic abuse. The PTGI scale was created to measure post-traumatic development, and it has given us important new understandings of how hardship may change us.

The PTGI, created by Tedeschi and Calhoun, is a self-report questionnaire with 21 questions measuring how much you believe you have improved since, in this case, going through narcissistic abuse.[2] These constructive adjustments cover a wide range of topics, such as inner fortitude, a deeper appreciation of life, strengthened bonds with others, increased spirituality or existential significance, and the pursuit of new opportunities.

Typically, the PTGI is made up of a number of statements or items that you rate according to your personal experiences. In order to reflect the changes you have gone through following narcissistic abuse, you indicate how much you agree or disagree with each statement. The PTGI assigns a score to you, indicating the degree of post-traumatic growth you have attained.

I've adapted the original questionnaire for you to complete below so you can see just how much post-traumatic growth you have experienced. I hazard a guess there will be some, however little. It's crucial to understand that the PTGI is a self-report measure of perceived growth rather than a diagnostic instrument. It comes from your subjective feelings about the questions.

THE PTGI QUESTIONNAIRE

This questionnaire is designed to help you assess your potential for personal growth and positive change following a traumatic experience. Please read each statement carefully and rate how much it applies to your current situation on a scale from 1 to 5, with 1 being 'not at all' and 5 being 'extremely.'

- I have a greater appreciation for life.

- I have discovered new possibilities in my life.

- I have developed a deeper sense of personal strength.

- I feel more connected to others.

- I have found a new sense of purpose or meaning in life.

Calculating your total score

Add up your scores for all five statements. The maximum possible score is 25, indicating the highest potential for post-traumatic growth.

Interpreting your results

- A score of 20–25 suggests a high potential for post-traumatic growth. You may be experiencing significant positive changes in your life as a result of your trauma.

- A score of 15–19 indicates moderate potential for growth. You are experiencing some positive changes but may benefit from further exploration.

- A score below 15 suggests lower potential for growth. Consider seeking support or engaging in activities that promote personal growth.

Reflecting on your progress

Use your score as a starting point for personal reflection and growth. Consider ways to harness your strengths and resilience to further your post-traumatic growth journey.

Remember that personal growth is a unique and ongoing process. Your results may change over time as you continue to heal and navigate the aftermath of your trauma. Use the PGTI as a tool for self-awareness and a guide to enhancing your well-being.

The emergence of the PTGI signaled a turning point in psychology by recognizing that hardship and growth could coexist, which helped to create a more comprehensive understanding of trauma's impact.

In the context of recovering from narcissistic abuse, the PTGI is particularly important. Narcissistic abuse is characterized by emotional control, harm to the mind, and psychological manipulation on the part of the narcissist. We frequently experience excruciating emotional suffering, damaged self-esteem, and a feeling of helplessness. The PTGI can be a useful resource for you as a survivor of narcissistic abuse in a number of ways:

Validation of personal growth

Survivors of narcissistic abuse can undervalue their own fortitude and development. The PTGI can support your sense of empowerment and self-worth by assisting you in recognizing and validating the good changes you have gone through.

Progress evaluation

The PTGI gives you a concrete means of evaluating your progress by giving you a way to measure your post-traumatic growth. This can be comforting, especially during the tough times in the recovery and healing process.

Focus on strengths

The PTGI encourages you to focus on your strengths, rather than only dwelling on the negative parts of your experience, by examining areas such as personal strength and improved connections.

The PTGI prompts you to consider many aspects of growth, assisting you in identifying areas where additional growth and healing may be helpful.

Communication with therapists

In order to aid your recovery process, many survivors of narcissistic abuse visit therapists like me. Giving a therapist access to your PTGI results can offer insightful guidance and inform their therapeutic approach. I'll often do the PTGI with my clients, because sometimes they don't realize that even though there may be darkness, there's very often some light and growth that we can quantifiably measure.

PTGI scores can assist you in establishing recovery objectives and monitoring your development over time as you can start to see your PTGI increase. Setting goals can inspire and motivate you, and strengthen your dedication to your healing process.

The PTGI ultimately acts as a ray of hope, reassuring you that recovering from narcissistic abuse can result in significant personal growth and constructive transformation. This is why it's so important to keep working on your trauma healing, but also to integrate positive psychology tools like this, so you can keep tracking and measuring your success.

I know it can seem paradoxical that narcissistic abuse can bring growth and benefits to your life, but it can wake you up from a life where you have just been existing, rather than thriving. Narcissistic abuse shines such a big spotlight on those inner child wounds – it forces you to look at them. We can then choose to keep living in the dark or be open to healing and growth, and this is exactly why you're here. For that, you should be so proud of yourself. Healing is not easy – to even think about growth and living a better life can feel both appealing and super scary all, at the same time.

Express Your Feelings

I want you to now think about your feelings and experience of narcissistic abuse in as much detail as you can. By writing down your emotions, you can validate your experiences and process and release pent-up feelings. Grab a journal, notebook, or a blank piece of paper and a pen.

- Set the stage: Find a peaceful, private space where you can focus without interruptions. Take a few deep breaths to center yourself.

- Set your intention: Before you begin writing, set an intention for this exercise. Tell yourself that you are creating a safe and nonjudgmental space to explore your emotions.

- Start writing: Begin by writing down your feelings and thoughts related to the narcissistic abuse you've experienced. Let your emotions flow freely onto the paper. Write as if you are having a conversation with yourself, with complete honesty.

- Express everything: Don't hold back. Express all your emotions, including anger, sadness, frustration, confusion, and any other feelings that come up. Write about specific incidents or moments that made you feel hurt or manipulated.

- Validate your experience: As you write, remind yourself that your feelings are valid. Narcissistic abuse is emotionally damaging, and it's normal to have strong reactions to it.

- Release anger: If you feel anger, express it on paper. Write about what makes you angry, who or what you are angry at, and how it feels to let this emotion out.

- Reflect: After you've expressed your feelings, take a moment to reflect. Notice any sense of relief or validation that comes from acknowledging your emotions.

- Breathe: Take a few deep breaths to center yourself.

This exercise helps you validate your experiences by acknowledging your emotions and reactions to the abuse. It reminds you that your feelings are real and valid. Writing down your feelings also allows you to release pent-up emotions, providing a sense of relief and catharsis. Expressive writing can help you gain clarity about your experiences and emotions, making it easier to understand and process them, as well as encouraging self-compassion as you acknowledge your strength and resilience in surviving the abuse. By confronting and processing your emotions in this way, you are taking a significant step toward healing from the emotional wounds of narcissistic abuse.

Remember that healing is a journey, and it's OK to revisit this exercise as needed. Over time, it can contribute to your emotional well-being and help you move forward with greater understanding and self-compassion.

Finding the benefit

Once you've written down all your expressions of feeling, focus on the positive aspects of the experience. Below are some questions to help guide you:

- How has the experience changed you?

- What has the experience taught you?

- How has the experience made you better equipped to meet similar challenges in the future?

- How do you feel that this experience has made you grow as a person?

These can be thought-provoking questions, but one benefit for me is that my ex-husband made me heal my codependency. Had I not worked on healing this, I can guarantee I would have made my children codependent on me, as my only sense of worth at one time was being a mother. This put so much pressure on my children to make me happy. This wasn't their responsibility, though, and my relationship with them now is so amazing. They know more now about relationships than I knew at 40 years old! They're both the kindest and most compassionate children, and the best thing is that they both know they are good enough simply for being themselves. I didn't feel this until I was in my 40s. This is a massive benefit of narcissistic abuse ,as it woke me up and I became a cycle-breaker.

> *Finding benefit in experiencing narcissistic abuse is*
> *when we truly step into a higher level of healing.*

Take some time now to write down all the benefits. Don't forget how far you've come, what you've learned along the way, and the fact that healing is an ever-evolving lifelong journey, because you're now going to stop abandoning yourself and start to proactively self-love as you step into your best future self.

I always used to ask myself, 'Why me? I'm a nice person and never want to hurt anyone, so why me?' As I started to heal, the question became, 'Why not me?' I had the power and the power alone to change this. Healing was not in changing the narcissist – as we've seen, they will never change – but in having the power to heal myself.

The Effects of Post-Traumatic Growth on the Rest of Your Life

Post-traumatic growth can have a significant impact on much more than just the immediate aftermath of narcissistic abuse; it can affect your life in a number of ways:

Resilience

When you experience post-traumatic growth, you will typically have greater resilience when faced with misfortune in the future. You have acquired coping mechanisms and resilience that give you the fortitude and agility to face obstacles in life.

Greater well-being

Post-traumatic growth is linked to better psychological health, life satisfaction, and general well-being. When post-traumatic growth occurs, you can frequently report feeling happier and more fulfilled in your life.

Positive relationships

The interpersonal development brought on by post-traumatic growth can result in relationships that are healthier and more meaningful. You may improve your ability to communicate, develop empathy in your relationships, and set and uphold limits and boundaries.

Personal satisfaction

Post-traumatic growth frequently inspires you to pursue your hobbies and objectives with fresh vigor. You might experience a greater feeling of fulfillment and purpose in your job, as a parent, in pastimes, and with interpersonal connections.

Legacy of resilience

Post-traumatic growth can impact and inspire future generations in a positive way. It's so true that when you heal yourself, you heal the next generation, and we know through the study of epigenetics that this can go down seven generations, so what you're doing now is not only for you. When you start to heal, you'll frequently act as an inspiration for resilience and personal progress, imparting your knowledge and fortitude to your family, children, and wider community.

BREAKING GENERATIONAL CYCLES OF TRAUMA

We've all heard the saying, 'Hurt people will hurt people,' and it couldn't be more true. When we carry unresolved pain and trauma, it often spills over into our relationships and interactions, both personally and professionally. But here's the incredible flip side of that coin: Healed people have the potential to heal others and break those chains of suffering.

On a personal level, healing allows us to build healthier relationships with our loved ones. We can nurture our children in an environment free from the shadow of generational trauma, offering them a brighter future.

Professionally, when we invest in our healing journey, it's not just about our own growth; it impacts our entire workspace. When we break free from the cycle of hurt, we become better communicators, empathetic leaders, and more supportive colleagues. Our work environments become healthier and more productive.

But it's not just about us. It's about creating a ripple effect of healing that can extend far beyond our immediate circles. When we heal, we become beacons of hope and inspiration for others who may be struggling in silence. We show them that transformation is possible, and we break down the stigma surrounding mental health. We can really start to see some generational shifts when we consistently work on our self-healing.

Post-traumatic growth is a powerful testament to the resilience of the human spirit. It reminds us that, even in our darkest hours, there is potential for transformation and growth. Embracing post-traumatic growth offers hope, not only for surviving narcissistic abuse, but for thriving in its aftermath, emerging stronger and more resilient than ever before. My wish for you in reading this book is that you'll start to experience post-traumatic growth.

In the end, post-traumatic growth serves as a reminder to us all that healing is possible and that, even in the most trying circumstances, there's always room for development and change.

In the next chapter, we'll explore how rewriting your story can feed into post-traumatic growth and take you closer to your happy ending.

CHAPTER 10

The Story of Your Healing

After narcissistic abuse, you can often internalize negative beliefs about yourself, such as feeling unworthy, unlovable, unimportant, or not good enough. These beliefs are reinforced by the gaslighting and manipulation tactics used by the narcissist. You may also develop harmful stories about your past, present, and future, such as feeling like a victim, expecting mistreatment from others, or believing you're doomed to repeat the same unhealthy patterns in your future relationships.

In this chapter, I want to explore a beautiful story that you can create with yourself right at the heart of it, as the hero(ine). Joseph Campbell, a renowned mythologist and scholar of comparative religion, introduced the concept of the Hero's Journey in his groundbreaking work, *The Hero with a Thousand Faces*.[1] Originally published in 1949, this book has had a profound influence on storytelling, literature, film, and our understanding of human narratives. The Hero's Journey is a universal storytelling framework that transcends cultural and historical boundaries, revealing the common threads that connect the myths and stories of different civilizations throughout time. I've included it in this book as I want you to start writing your own story – and you get to choose the ending.

Narcissistic abuse can leave us with deep emotional wounds, shattered self-esteem, and a distorted sense of self. Using the Hero's Journey can be a powerful tool for healing because it addresses the negative thought patterns and stories that often emerge after such a traumatic relationship. The Hero's Journey is a narrative framework that reflects the human experience of growth, transformation, and overcoming adversity. It involves a hero who faces challenges, learns, and emerges stronger – yes, that's you.

By using the Hero's Journey as a metaphor for your own journey, you can reframe your experience. You can see yourself as the hero, not the victim, of your own story, with the power to overcome challenges and find strength within. The Hero's Journey can help you break free from the victim mentality that narcissistic abuse often instills. It encourages you to take ownership of your narrative and move from a place of powerlessness to empowerment. This all contributes to you stepping into your best future self and into post-traumatic growth.

The Hero's Journey Framework

At the core of Joseph Campbell's Hero's Journey is the idea that myths and stories from diverse cultures share a fundamental structure. Campbell proposed that these stories, whether from ancient Greece, Native American folklore, or African legends, follow a similar pattern. This pattern consists of a hero's transformative journey, marked by various stages, trials, and revelations. In films and books, there's a beginning, a middle, and an end, and a flow to the story as we watch or read. However, the Hero's Journey is not a rigid formula, but rather a flexible framework that you can use to create a compelling narrative of your experiences so far and where you want your life to be. It provides a template for understanding the hero's evolution from an ordinary individual to one experiencing trauma and narcissistic abuse, to a transformed and enlightened figure.

This journey is rich in psychological and spiritual symbolism, making it a powerful tool for exploring your human experience of narcissistic abuse and your healing transformation, even if you're just starting out on your healing journey. When we apply this framework to healing from narcissistic abuse, writing your story can sometimes give a sense of embarking on a different path toward your happy ending.

By writing your own personal life story, you can do two things:

1. You can celebrate how far you've come. So often, we're only focusing on where we think we should be, but even if you're only just starting your healing journey, that in itself is cause for celebration. You bought this book, right?

2. You can embrace the opportunity to really see the greatness within you and start to prime yourself for the future you deserve. When we start to write and visualize a future we want, we're already starting to change our body chemistry to make that future happen. Some people call this 'The Secret' or manifestation, but there's science behind this.[2] You get to be the director of your life. Sometimes that can seem scary and while we don't know what the future may look like or who will be in it, this journey gives you the chance to explore and know what is possible. *And it is possible.* I'm living proof of that.

Key elements of the Hero's Journey

Campbell identified several key elements that recur in Hero's Journey narratives. Below is a short breakdown of the chapters in your story and then I'll explain them in more detail so you can start to write your story of survival, healing, and thriving:

1. The call to adventure: The hero receives a call or summons to embark on a quest or journey. This call may come from an external source or arise from an internal desire for change or adventure.

2. The refusal of the call: Initially, the hero may resist this call for healing due to fear, doubt, or a sense of inadequacy. This reluctance often serves to highlight the hero's humanity and vulnerability: 'I'm not worthy or good enough.'

3. Meeting the mentor: The hero encounters a wise mentor or guide who provides guidance, training, and support. This mentor helps the hero overcome challenges and grow. (This could even be the fact you've bought this book!)

4. Crossing the threshold: This is when the hero leaves their ordinary world and enters a new, unfamiliar one. This transition symbolizes a significant change and sets the hero on the path of transformation.

5. Tests, allies, and enemies: Throughout the journey, the hero faces a series of trials, meets allies, and confronts adversaries (like the narcissist or family members who don't believe you). These experiences help the hero develop skills, gather resources, and gain self-awareness.

6. Approaching the inmost cave: The hero moves closer to the heart of their quest, often encountering the most significant

challenges and dangers. This stage represents a deep inner and outer reckoning. (For you, this could be the court process, a divorce, or challenging parents.)

7. The ordeal: This is when the hero undergoes a profound test, battle, or inner crisis. This is often a moment of life-or-death significance, where their mettle and character are tested to the fullest. (For me, this was when I had over $90,000 of debt and was made homeless.)

8. The reward: After overcoming the ordeal, the hero reaps the rewards, which might include newfound knowledge, wisdom, or a tangible prize. (This reward is often what you have set out to obtain: post-traumatic growth.)

9. The road back: The hero begins the journey back to the ordinary world but may face further challenges or confrontations with enemies or inner demons.

10. The resurrection: In the final confrontation, the hero experiences a symbolic death and rebirth. This transformation represents their transcendence and growth.

11. Returning with the elixir: The hero returns to the ordinary world, bringing back the wisdom, knowledge, or gift acquired during the journey. This return often benefits their community or society.

The Hero's Journey is not merely a framework for storytelling; it also holds deep psychological and cultural significance. Campbell argued that these stories resonate with audiences because they mirror our own personal journeys through life. The hero's challenges, growth, and ultimate triumph reflect the human experience of facing obstacles, seeking meaning, and striving for self-realization. This is why I have written my own personal Heroine's Journey and would love to invite you to do the same.

You may be at different stages and chapters along the way, but my hope for you is that, by doing this, you can see how far you have come, where you are right now, and that keeping focused on your own self-healing can give you hope and post-traumatic growth to live your life as your best future self. It allows you to journal all of your past, acknowledge your present, and envision hope and action for the future.

The Hero's Journey offers insights into our own quests for meaning, self-discovery, and personal evolution as we experience narcissistic abuse. It reminds us that the stories we tell are a reflection of our shared humanity and the timeless quest to find purpose and fulfillment in our lives.

The Hero's Journey can be a powerful framework for survivors of narcissistic abuse to process our experiences and embark on a path of healing and recovery. Remember, this may not have happened yet at all for you, but we're priming your system for healing and growth.

Narcissistic abuse is a complex and devastating form of emotional and psychological mistreatment that can leave victims feeling trapped, isolated, and powerless. Survivors often describe it as a soul-crushing experience that shatters their self-esteem and sense of self-worth. However, just as in Joseph Campbell's Hero's Journey, those who have endured narcissistic abuse can embark on a transformative journey toward healing, self-discovery, and empowerment.

So, let's explore how you could start to write your own Hero's Journey and use it as a map of post-traumatic growth and self-healing. Below I'll explain how each stage of the Hero's Journey can be adapted to address narcissistic abuse and guide you in writing your own story of survival and growth. By weaving the Hero's Journey into your healing process, you can find the strength and resilience to not only recover but also emerge from this trauma as an empowered individual, ready to share your wisdom and to support others in their journeys to healing.

The Hero's Journey through Narcissistic Abuse

Grab yourself a journal and a pen, or a digital device, and start writing your own Hero(ine)'s Journey.

The call to adventure: acknowledging the abuse

Your journey begins with the call to adventure, which is the recognition that you're in an abusive relationship. This moment often emerges from a deep sense of unease, as you start to recognize the signs of narcissistic abuse. Acknowledging the abuse is a pivotal step toward healing. This is why you should be so proud that you have bought this book – awareness is key.

In this chapter of your story, you can describe the initial signs that raised red flags, such as subtle manipulations, inconsistencies in the narcissist's behavior, or feelings of unease and confusion. Start to reflect on what finally led you to accept that you were in an abusive relationship and considered seeking help. It's a validation chapter for you in looking at all the things you can now see. Don't worry if you feel it's just the start of your healing – do what you can, because, like any good writer, you can go back and edit. This is *your* Hero's Journey.

The refusal of the call: denial and fear

After acknowledging the abuse, you may experience a period of denial and fear. 'Is it me?' 'Am I the narcissist?' 'Is it my fault?' This takes you all the way back to what we've been learning in the previous chapters. You may struggle with the idea that someone you loved and trusted could be intentionally harming you. You have such kindness in your soul that you can't understand how a human being could treat another human being like this. This stage involves self-doubt and the internal resistance to accepting the painful reality.

Writing this chapter involves recounting the emotional turmoil and self-doubt that may be keeping you in that trapped state of denial. You can start to explore what made you hesitant to confront the truth – think back to the previous chapters in this book where we discussed attachment, nervous system and safety, your protector response, and your childhood. Your chapter might include fear of the unknown, feelings of guilt, or the dread of facing the harsh consequences of the truth.

Meeting the mentor: seeking support

This is when you reach out for help or information, often connecting with a therapist, support group, a trusted friend, or even me and this book. They become your mentor in the journey toward self-healing. This mentor helps you navigate the complex emotions and challenges you face during narcissistic abuse recovery.

Writing this chapter involves describing the moment of seeking support and the impact it had on your path to recovery. What was that pivotal moment, when you knew you needed support? It's an opportunity to share how the mentor's guidance, insights, and validation are playing a crucial role in your healing journey.

Crossing the threshold: leaving the narcissist

This stage marks your decision to leave the narcissistic relationship, whether it's a physical departure or an emotional detachment, and whether that be a romantic partner, parent, friend, or coworker.

Writing this chapter should include the process of planning and executing your departure, which can be a complex and challenging task. Think about what boundaries need to be put in place – for example, around your finances, children, navigating ageing parents, and so on. You can share the difficulties you've faced, such as the narcissist's attempts to manipulate or control you, the fear of retaliation, and the emotional turmoil of severing ties with someone you once cared deeply for.

Tests, allies, and enemies: building a support system

As you take steps toward recovery, you begin to establish relationships with allies who support your healing journey. These allies can be therapists, support groups like my free Facebook group (see *Resources, page 239*), friends, or family members who provide guidance, validation, and emotional support. This can be challenging as it will make you look at everyone through a different lens, so take some time here. As we've seen, often when healing from narcissistic abuse we need to go through a 'friends cleanse,' so your circle may initially get smaller (see *page 187*). But remember, this is your life, and you're starting to create the life you deserve.

Writing this chapter involves introducing key allies and describing how they may play a role in your self-healing journey. It's a chance to reflect on the challenges encountered, including the pushback or manipulation from the narcissist or their enablers.

Approaching the inmost cave: facing trauma

Your inner journey is where you confront the emotional and psychological trauma caused by the abuse. This stage represents a deep dive into the painful memories, feelings of powerlessness, and the process of acknowledging the depth of the scars left by the abuser – all the stuff we've explored in previous chapters. Remember, this needs to be done slowly (we call this titration) – if you go too fast at this point and don't give your body space, you'll keep staying in freeze.

In this chapter, you can explore the healing experiences that are helping you process your trauma. It's an opportunity to shed light on the darkest corners of your journey and how you have confronted your pain.

The ordeal: healing and self-discovery

The ordeal stage represents your journey of healing and self-discovery. This is where you undergo deep healing, engage in self-care, and work on reclaiming your identity and true self.

While writing this chapter, focus on the strategies, tools, and inner strength you've found to overcome the trauma of narcissistic abuse and rebuild your life. This is the start of seeing some light and coming out of the fog. You can detail your healing process, discussing the healing techniques that have helped you most, such as IMF, somatic experiencing, nervous system regulation, breathwork, meditations, and positive psychology, as well as the support you've received from loved ones, and how you began to reconnect with your authentic and true self. It's an opportunity to convey the immense effort and resilience required for healing.

The reward: empowerment and growth

In this chapter, you can recount the rewards and transformations you have experienced through your healing journey. The rewards might include increased self-esteem, a greater sense of fulfillment and purpose, and newfound resilience. Think back to everything we discussed about awakening to post-traumatic growth. You can discuss the moments of self-discovery, newly discovered strengths, positive changes, and the emerging sense of empowerment that came with healing. You can also reflect on how your perspective on life and relationships has evolved.

The road back: moving forward

This is when you're embarking on the journey toward a new beginning. Writing this chapter should describe how you have taken steps to move forward, possibly by setting new goals, rebuilding relationships, and pursuing your passions. You can share the strategies you've used to create a brighter future, such as setting boundaries, practicing self-care, and engaging in personal development. It's a chance to highlight the resilience and determination that have propelled you forward. Not just bouncing back, but bouncing forward.

The resurrection: reclaiming power

The resurrection stage represents your final confrontation with your past, where you fully break free from the lingering effects of narcissistic abuse. Writing this chapter involves illustrating how you have reclaimed your power, self-worth, and control over your life. You can reflect on the inner strength you have discovered during your healing journey and how you've used it to overcome triggers, residual trauma, or any attempts by the narcissist to reassert control. This stage symbolizes your rebirth and triumph over your past.

Returning with the elixir: sharing wisdom

In this final chapter, you get to share the wisdom gained from your journey of healing. It's an opportunity to offer guidance, support, and inspiration to others who may be experiencing or recovering from narcissistic abuse. It's a way of giving back and helping those on similar paths. You can discuss the importance of raising awareness about narcissistic abuse, the signs to watch out for, and the resources available for support. You can convey a message of hope and resilience, emphasizing that healing is possible and that survivors can emerge from their ordeal as empowered individuals.

See the possibilities of turning darkness into light, struggle into strength, and even pain into purpose.

The Hero's Journey framework offers a powerful narrative structure for you as a survivor of narcissistic abuse to process your experiences and navigate the path to healing and empowerment. By breaking down your journey into distinct stages, you can better understand your own resilience and the significance of each step in your recovery.

The Hero's Journey through narcissistic abuse is not only a personal narrative but also a testament to the human spirit's capacity to overcome adversity. When you share your survivor story, wherever that may be right now, you contribute to raising awareness of the dynamics of narcissistic abuse, and offer invaluable support and inspiration to others who are on similar journeys. We heal together and together we can reenvision narcissism.

The Hero's Journey through narcissistic abuse is a testament to your strength, resilience, and capacity for growth. By writing your own personal Hero's Journey with this framework, you can find your voice, reclaim your power, and ultimately emerge as a hero in your own narrative of healing and transformation.

With your story rewritten, it's time to step into your best future self.

CHAPTER 11

Your Best Future Self

In this final chapter, we'll pull together all your key learnings from the book and step into your best future self. We'll also look at a final piece of this journey – self-forgiveness and self-actualization. You'll realize that you can now safely come home to your body, ready to live your best life – a life you deserve and always have – and you'll understand that other people's behavior is never a reflection of you.

Narcissistic abuse happened TO you and at no point ever BECAUSE of you.

Moving from post-traumatic stress to post-traumatic growth is probably one of the hardest journeys you'll ever have to go through, but if you keep committed to yourself, it can be the most powerful transformation you'll ever experience. You deserve happiness; you deserve a life that is filled with love and connection. It is all available; it's just about staying committed to the healing journey.

When you're committed to healing and recovery, you can start on a deep and life-altering path toward self-actualization. This entails taking charge once again, repairing damaged self-esteem, and accepting your true self.

The Life-Changing Effects of Self-Actualization

Self-actualization describes the journey toward reaching one's fullest potential and actualizing one's greatest self. In the context of narcissistic abuse, it means working toward all of our protector parts being as calm as they can be, so that we can step into our true self and feel safe to be seen and heard, simply for being who we are at our core. Self-actualization is crucial to recovery from narcissistic abuse because, as you've learned, the journey is multilayered. You have never been broken; you have just felt unsafe being yourself, which led to nervous system dysregulation and protector responses. Your inner system has done an amazing job of trying to keep you as safe and emotionally pain-free as possible, but now is your time to step into your healing and your greatness because you are simply amazing just for being *you*.

Abraham Maslow developed the concept of self-actualization as the top level in his hierarchy of needs.[1] If someone's physiological, safety, social, and esteem needs are met, Maslow says that person can then move on to the next level of development, which is self-actualization. In the context of this book, once we have worked on our past, understood that none of it was our fault, learned to build nervous system capacity and flexibility so we can stay in the ventral vagal and be present in our life, we are then safe to live as our true self.

When you strive for self-actualization, it pushes you to rediscover and accept your unique true self. Think of your true self as the sunshine and your protector response as the clouds. Just because the clouds and protector response are there, it doesn't mean the sunshine has gone – it's just behind the clouds.

The road to self-actualization after surviving narcissistic abuse is a winding one, fraught with setbacks and difficulties at every turn. But this is life, and we have to understand that healing is not a magical destination – it's a journey, and one we should keep pursuing all of our life because, as we reach a new level, there will always be a new devil.

> *Don't set yourself up for failure setting*
> *destinations – just keep taking one day at*
> *a time because that is good enough.*

Self-actualization is impossible without the acceptance and awareness that the abuse occurred, understanding that getting better will take time, and realizing that it's time to stop abandoning yourself and step into self-love. Realizing this can be both difficult and freeing. The journey to self-actualization is one of introspection and learning about oneself. It's a beautiful self-healing journey. Self-actualization is a challenging path, but it's not one that you must walk alone. Yes, only you can do the work as all healing is self-healing, but you're not alone on this journey. I'm right by your side.

Self-actualization helps you navigate the challenging terrain of recovery, allowing you to emerge stronger, more self-aware, and ultimately more fulfilled. It has so many benefits for us all.

Taking back control
Narcissists feed off dominating and controlling you. Self-actualization is a process that helps you realize that you're

capable of making decisions and influencing your own life after experiencing trauma.

Narcissistic abuse is devastating to your sense of self-worth, which must be rebuilt over time. Recognizing and appreciating your individual talents and skills is an important part of the self-actualization process that can help restore your sense of worth, because we get lost along the way literally just trying to survive.

Those who have achieved a high level of self-actualization, and feel safe living simply for being who they are, are more likely to bounce back quickly from setbacks as they have built more resilience. This is why narcissistic abuse can be a gift when we embrace our healing as the narcissist shines a big spotlight on wounds that are already present and feeds into them. Healing from narcissistic abuse can bring more inner strength and coping mechanisms to overcome the obstacles you may face on the road to recovery from abuse and for the rest of your life.

I still work on myself every day because I deserve it. I no longer abandon myself and say I'm too busy. I need to be my priority so I can show up as the best version of myself – for me, my family, and my amazing community of people just like you.

Boundary establishment

Learning to set healthy boundaries is an important part of reaching your full potential and protecting yourself from further abuse and exploitation. You'll now have set your boundaries and named those who are in your inner circle and those who are in the outer circle (see page 96). When we have core emotional wounds, we often end up spending more time with those in the outer circle as we want to prove our worth, yet it should be the complete opposite.

Relationship repair

The path to self-actualization can pave the way to happier, more rewarding interactions with others. Often when we're healing, we see people as dangerous because there's a potential that they can hurt us, but that's because we're carrying a wounded inner child.

When we can change the somatic experience of our inner child, we start to look back and not blend with our wounds, and we're able to start to feel safe as who we truly are. We can see now that our wounds merely came from our interpretation of events and people from our childhood. The ability to make true connections with others improves with the more self-healing we do, and as we develop greater authenticity and self-awareness.

Narcissists often use cunning tactics to isolate you from your loved ones as they want you to become totally reliant on them as their source of narcissistic supply. They can use finances in particular to do that. They may subtly undermine your confidence, manipulate your perceptions, and sow seeds of doubt about the intentions of your friends and family.

Over time, you might find yourself withdrawing from those who care about you, feeling increasingly alone and dependent on the narcissist for validation and money. However, as you begin to heal, you can regain the clarity to recognize these manipulative tactics and start to reconnect with family and friends. This involves rebuilding trust, reestablishing boundaries, and rediscovering the warmth of genuine connections.

Take comfort in knowing that you are not alone
in your journey toward healing and reconnection.

Self-forgiveness

We can feel such rage and anger as we start to heal, and our inner critic part can show up again asking, 'How could you be so stupid?' Forgiveness is a huge part of our healing journey. But forgiveness is maybe not what you think. Many people may say that the narcissist is a wounded individual and, to truly heal, you must forgive them. This isn't true; it's actually a gaslighting statement making you believe that you must do this to heal and that, if you're not healing, then in some way this is your fault. It's not. None of this is your fault and you never deserved to be treated like this.

Forgiveness is actually about forgiving the younger version of yourself who didn't know better. The reason you didn't know better wasn't because you're weak or stupid, it's because you were never taught. Who teaches us about attachment, our nervous system, our brain? No one. This is why I'm so passionate about my Trauma-Informed Coaching Certification – I can see my students and graduates taking this work into the world to create a ripple effect.

Self-forgiveness is a learned skill and can feel heavy after experiencing narcissistic abuse because you may struggle and fall into the trap of telling yourself things like, 'I don't deserve forgiveness,' 'I deserve to feel this guilt,' or 'I'm just a bad person.' You can't stop hurting yourself if you refuse to forgive yourself. It's a key part of healing. Our critical part may not want to leave us as it serves the purpose of keeping us vigilant, but this keeps elevated levels of cortisol in the body, which leads to disease and illness.

When you forgive yourself, you're not trying to forget, condone, or excuse anyone's act. Nor are you trying to avoid feelings of regret and remorse. Acknowledging narcissistic abuse, expressing regret, and improving our nervous system regulation and behaviors are key components of this process. Forgiving yourself is another step toward moving past any mistake, big or small, and learning not to repeat it. I found self-forgiveness hard initially as I was really critical of myself and some of the decisions and actions I made along the way. My ex-husband had made me behave in ways that I was ashamed of – getting angry and snapping all the time. I had learned to hate myself, but I needed to forgive myself and you do too.

Write a self-forgiveness letter

I want you to get two pieces of paper and a pen. On one piece of paper, with your nondominant writing hand, write a letter to yourself sharing all the things you feel hurt about – any shame, any choices and decisions you made – and how you feel about them all. Start it with 'Dear Adult Self' and sign off 'Younger Self.' Then take some time to read this letter. Notice the sensations that come up. You may want to hold yourself as if you were giving yourself a hug to feel a connection, like someone is there for you. Let any tears flow as you write and read this.

Then, on the second piece of paper, with your dominant writing hand, I want you to write a letter to yourself and start it 'Dear Younger Self.' I want you to tell that wounded, younger part of yourself everything they need to hear with your newfound understanding from working through all the chapters in this book. Give lots of praise, lots of explanations, and always point out that this was not their fault. Narcissistic abuse does not define them – it's something that has happened to them and is never a reflection of themselves or their worth. Sign this letter, 'With love from Adult Self.' This is a powerful exercise, so don't underestimate how much emotion it will bring up.

Writing the first letter allows you to validate your inner child's experiences and writing the second letter, from your adult self, allows you to step into more compassion and understanding. Writing a self-forgiveness letter like this is a powerful tool for self-reflection, emotional release, and personal growth. You can gain self-awareness, empathy toward yourself, and a sense of closure, which helps you move toward self-forgiveness and, ultimately, leads to improved mental and emotional well-being.

The benefits of this exercise are profound:

- Self-awareness: When you sit down to write a self-forgiveness letter, you are forced to confront your actions, mistakes, and the emotions associated with them. This process fosters self-awareness as you delve into your feelings of guilt, regret, and remorse.

- Emotional catharsis: The act of putting feelings into words on paper can be cathartic. It allows you to release pent-up emotions, providing a sense of relief and emotional release.

- Reflection and accountability: Writing a self-forgiveness letter encourages you to take responsibility for your actions and be kind to your younger self who didn't know better. As the adult, you can objectively evaluate the situation and acknowledge the past.

- Empathy toward yourself: Through the process of self-forgiveness, you can learn to extend the same empathy and understanding to yourself that you might offer to others. You begin to recognize that you are human, and are capable of making mistakes and finding yourself in challenging situations.

- Healing and closure: The act of writing a self-forgiveness letter can contribute to a sense of healing and closure. It allows you to let go of the emotional burdens you've been carrying, leading to a lighter emotional load.

- Personal growth: Self-forgiveness is a crucial aspect of personal growth. By forgiving yourself, you can release the past and make room for self-improvement, enabling different choices in the future.

- Improved mental health: Self-forgiveness is associated with improved mental health outcomes, including reduced stress, anxiety, and depression.[2] It can lead to greater overall well-being.

- Encouragement for positive change: As you move toward self-forgiveness, you're more likely to engage in behaviors and thought patterns that align with self-compassion and personal growth.

Seeing your experience through the eyes of the adult you are today, as opposed to your wounded inner child, can bring about real change. You'll see that this was all in the past; you're safe now and have more power and choices.

Looking to the Future

Very often, when I'm working with my clients, I ask them what they would like in their future and 99 per cent tell me exactly what they *don't* want: a cheating partner, a narcissist in their life, to ever feel like this again. Most really struggle to think about what life could look like moving forward and what they actually *do* want. It almost feels alien to feel hope for a better life because the potential for more pain seems too great.

This goes back to the self-sabotaging protector response wanting to keep you vigilant for any danger. If you take your eye off the ball and dare to think about a future of joy, love, and connection, that could mean it could be taken away again and deposit you right back where you were. The problem with this is that we'll never ever open our eyes to the potential of possibilities, and this is exactly what this book is about – honoring your past, healing the trauma, and living your best life as your true self, feeling safe to do so.

I know that the future can seem a scary place after narcissistic abuse and it can feel like your life is over, but it's not. The positive psychology exercise below will help you start to envision what your life could be like as your best possible future self.

YOUR BEST FUTURE SELF

Pick a future date when your actions will have an impact, but not so far in the future that you feel like it doesn't matter what you do now. It could be in six months, a year, or even three years from now – a time when you want to feel at ease and be living in peace with a regulated nervous system. Close your eyes, take a few deep, steady breaths, and believe that everything has gone as smoothly as it possibly could. You're thriving despite the inevitable ups and downs of life. As you do this, ask yourself:

- What motivates you to spring out of bed every morning, to dive headfirst into the day when you first open your eyes?

- How does this help you get closer to the life you envision for yourself?

- How are you making daily investments in your health to make this a reality?

- In what ways are you able to fit these routines into your daily life?

- How does this affect your relationships?

- How are you feeling as a result of this?

- How does your care for yourself benefit those around you, like your children or family?

- How have your family and friends responded to the new you?

- Why are all of these actions so important for you? It may be to make you a better parent or to make you feel healthier and able to do more.

- What about these actions has made your loved ones so happy?

Make your mental picture of this future as clear and detailed as you can. We're working your brain and body to prime you for this life and to believe that it is possible.

Now, write all of this down like it's a done deal. This is now your life, and you're living it as your best future self. Record what you have written down into your phone or recording device and keep listening to it every single day.

This will enable you to visualize your new life and help your body feel that it's safe to live it like this. The power of visualization and listening to this recording each day means you are literally priming yourself for when, not if, it happens. It is all available and possible for you.

The Healing Power of Gratitude After Narcissistic Abuse

We've already explored how gratitude is a powerful emotion that can help you focus on the bright side of life and your own recovery when we looked at the positive psychology interventions in Chapter 7. Those of us who have suffered at the hands of a narcissist can begin the journey toward healing and flourishing by cultivating an attitude of appreciation. By doing so, we not only help ourselves recover, but also generate a wave of positivity and community solidarity.

I'm extremely grateful for my ex-husband, who woke me up to realize what is truly important. I know this will be hard for some of you, but remember this is never about excusing the abuse you have gone through. It's about recognizing the good when there is bad.

There will always be light with the dark, so we can truly appreciate the light as and when it happens.

Of course, I'm not saying that how my ex-husband treated me was OK – on the contrary – but I would never have done the inner work or experienced the deep sense of self-healing had I not met and married him. I would be living a mediocre life, which would have been OK, but life is so precious and I want to really live it, at all levels, and not just exist.

Post-traumatic growth after narcissistic abuse turns how we think about trauma upside down. I know this can be hard to get your head around right now, but I promise if you keep committing to yourself and your healing journey, at some point the gratitude will come and you will have stepped into an even higher level of post-traumatic growth.

Those who have survived narcissistic abuse can benefit so much from continuing to cultivate an attitude of gratitude, as it's a powerful and transformational emotion. I want to now delve into the significant role that gratitude plays in recovery and flourishing in the wake of abuse, and offer a positive psychology practice designed to move you beyond the little gratitude habits we explored on page 150 so you can foster appreciation and usher in a life of flourishing.

THE POSITIVE CONSEQUENCES OF EXPRESSING THANKS

Beyond physical health, thankfulness has far-reaching advantages. Gratitude can have a domino effect on the relationships and communities of narcissistic abuse survivors.

Relationships benefit from grateful people because they're more empathetic, forgiving, and understanding. We've all been in a room where someone just lights it up. I know I used to be like a dementor! I could have sucked the joy out of the happiest of occasions, whereas now, I like to think that I bring joy to those around me. As a result of this, you may find that your connections with those closest to you improve and flourish.

A sense of belonging can also be fostered through gratitude among narcissistic abuse survivors. Mutual support and encouragement might result from sharing accounts of thankfulness and successful recovery. This is really felt in my free Facebook support group (see *Resources, page 239*).

In addition, thankful people are more likely to help improve the lives of those around them and the world at large. As a result, you may feel inspired to do good deeds for others, which has a multiplicative effect on wellness.

Practicing gratitude

Appreciation exercises based on positive psychology can help you tap into the healing power of gratitude and go past survival toward flourishing. Here are four basic steps:

Step 1: Think back on your experiences of narcissistic abuse

Find a place of peace and comfort where you can start processing your past, especially the hurt and difficulties associated with narcissistic abuse. Feel free to experience all of the feelings that come with those memories. Let the tears flow.

Step 2: Compile a list of thanks

This may seem hard at first — and if this is too tough right now, always know that you can come back to this exercise at any point as you keep committed to your self-healing. After reflecting on your history of narcissistic abuse, turn your attention to counting your blessings. These may be trivial or crucial. Think about these questions:

- What have been the happiest times in your life?

- Who have been your biggest cheerleaders and biggest advocates?

- What do you find most admirable about yourself?

- In light of your current situation of trying to heal from narcissistic abuse, what are you most grateful for?

Jot down the things for which you are thankful as they come to mind. Don't just describe something vaguely; try to describe it precisely.

Step 3: Show your appreciation

Use the reasons for appreciation you've uncovered in a way that makes sense to you. Keeping a gratitude notebook, verbalizing your gratitude aloud, or writing thank-you notes are all great ways to achieve this.

You may, for instance, acknowledge your resilience and inner strength by penning a letter to yourself. Another option is to show appreciation to a loved one or close friend who has helped you become well.

Step 4: Make gratitude a regular habit

Make a habit out of expressing thanks every day. Keeping a thankfulness diary in which you record at least three things for which you are thankful daily can help. You could start by committing to a daily or nightly practice of counting your blessings – sometimes they will be big and sometimes they will be small. Research has shown that expressing three different gratitudes every day can turn a pessimist into a mild optimist, so there is hope.[3]

I practice daily gratitude before I get out of bed. A more cheerful and hopeful view can be fostered through a regular thankfulness practice – your brain can't be angry and grateful at the same time. Healing and moving on from the wounds left by narcissistic abuse are processes that get easier with time.

Narcissistic abuse is an insidious form of domestic abuse which is trauma. It doesn't happen overnight; it slowly chips away at the core of who you are. But through these chapters and all the interventions and exercises, you're hopefully now starting to see that there is light at the end of the tunnel, and you can step into post-traumatic growth. Bringing together all that you have learned as you've journeyed through this book will enable you to step into your best possible future self.

CONCLUSION:
HEALING AND THRIVING

I'm incredibly proud of you for embarking on this journey of healing after narcissistic abuse. Your dedication and courage in confronting the emotional wounds inflicted by such a challenging experience is truly admirable. It takes immense strength to delve into the depths of your emotions, process the pain, and work toward reclaiming your self-worth and well-being. Your commitment to your own healing is a testament to your resilience and determination, and you should be immensely proud of yourself.

Remember, healing is a profound and transformative journey, and you are taking each step with grace and strength. Your progress is an inspiration, and your journey toward recovery is a testament to your inner strength and unwavering spirit. Keep moving forward; you are deserving of all the happiness and peace that await you on this path of healing. Pause for a moment, be proud, and celebrate how far you have come.

This book has taken you on a voyage of self-discovery. You now know what your attachment style is and how you can keep working to make it secure. Understanding your nervous system and what protector responses you have can be so helpful in releasing shame and knowing there are no bad parts of you – even the destructive parts are still trying to help you move away and soothe you from an internal pain that was interpreted from childhood.

You now have a much deeper understanding of your childhood – and you are a cycle breaker. Many people experience narcissistic abuse and never go through this healing process. You are here and this is huge. Life is going to improve as you start to step into your post-traumatic growth and release the past in your readiness for a new and exciting future.

This book is not to be read once and never come back to. It's a book to be read over and over again – I truly believe you can use this as your healing bible for now and in the future. This work is a lifelong journey, but narcissistic abuse gave you the key to start it, and you deserve to stay on it so you never abandon yourself ever again.

Narcissistic abuse does not define who you are. It's an experience you have adapted to. Now it's time to step into the light and live the life you truly deserve as you heal, thrive, and flourish after narcissistic abuse. Now is the time to stop abandoning yourself, commit to self-love, and shift from post-traumatic stress to post-traumatic growth after the trauma of narcissistic abuse.

You, my friend, deserve to heal,
thrive, and flourish.

Keep working on yourself and remember you're not alone on this journey. We heal together. I'm right by your side. Come and find me on social media and join my free support group (*see Resources, page 239*). It may seem hard, but it's so worth it.

You are enough.

You are worthy.

You are lovable.

You are important.

You always have been, you are now, and you always will be.

Now is your time to shine.

FIFTEEN COMMON TERMS IN THE WORLD OF NARCISSISTIC ABUSE

Baiting

A narcissist loves to provoke a reaction from you, especially in public. They will provoke you into responding in an angry or emotional manner. (Your angry response is then further 'evidence' of your unbalanced state of mind.)

Boundaries

A code of conduct or an unwritten set of rules that we consider to be reasonable behavior from those around us, and our response when someone steps over the line. Narcissists DO NOT respect boundaries and will get angry if you try to set or enforce them.

Closure

In a normal relationship, closure involves open and honest communication about what has gone wrong, you wish each other well, say goodbye, and move on. After a relationship with a narcissist ends, the target is left with so many questions and no answers. It feels like the book has been closed before the story has ended. We cannot expect any form of closure from the emotionally immature narcissist, who is completely lacking in empathy, with no regard for your feelings. The only closure in this type of relationship is the closure you give yourself.

Codependent

The individual characteristics vary from person to person. Some of the more common characteristics include trying to avoid making decisions, preferring to rely on others. Codependents are often perfectionists who tend to put the needs of others above their own.

Flying monkeys

People who have been convinced by the narcissist that it's the narcissist who is actually the victim. Flying monkeys inflict further harm on the real victim by submitting to the narcissist's wishes and demands. They may threaten, torment, discredit, or add fuel to a smear campaign by spreading lies and gossip.

Gaslighting

A manipulative tactic where a mentally healthy individual is subjected to conditioning behavior so that they doubt their own sanity. The target starts to believe that their perception of reality is false. The narcissist may simply deny something happened when it did, tell you that you heard wrong, or lie about an event or situation. Over time, a victim starts to think they are confused and going crazy. They come to rely more and more on the narcissist.

Hoovering

Describes how a narcissist attempts to suck their victims back into a relationship. They will use every trick in the book to get you back under their power and control. Hoovering often takes place after you have left them or after a period of silent treatment. They often promise to change their behavior or say that they have already changed dramatically.

Invalidation

A manipulative tactic used to get the target to believe that their thoughts, opinions, and beliefs are wrong, unimportant, or don't matter.

Love bombing

A term used to describe the typical initial stages of a relationship where the narcissist goes all-out to impress their target with flattery, holidays, and promises of a future together, having the target believe that they have met their perfect partner, their soulmate.

Mirroring

A narcissist will mirror what they see in you, from your mannerisms to your dress sense, your behavior, and your likes and dislikes. They basically become just like you.

Narcissistic supply

A narcissist is lost without narcissistic supply. They need supply like a plant needs water. Supply consists of attention, admiration, respect, adulation, and even fear. Without these vital nutrients of life, the narcissist will become dysfunctional.

No contact

Put in place by a victim in order to give themselves time to recover. It is not in any way similar to the narcissist's silent treatment. A narcissist who initiates the silent treatment is doing so as a punishment and to exert power and control. No contact is a self-imposed set of rules whereby there will be absolutely no contact with the toxic person (no texts, no emails, no phone calls, no snooping on social media). It has been likened to building a wall between you and a toxic individual. You will not care or even be aware of what happens on the other side of this wall. (Extreme modified contact is advised if you have children with the narcissist.)

Projection

A narcissist is an expert at projecting their own character flaws or bad behavior onto others. They will not hold themselves accountable for any wrongdoing and will blame others for the very things that they do themselves. The main objective is to make themselves feel superior.

Self-esteem

The overall judgment one holds about one's own self-worth, which includes pride in oneself, self-respect, and self-assurance.

Trauma bonding

A misplaced loyalty where a victim is emotionally bonded with their abuser and finds themselves unable to leave an unhealthy or dangerous relationship. The victim remains loyal to someone who has betrayed them time and time again.

RESOURCES

For more support or information, follow me on Instagram, Facebook, or TikTok (@carolinestrawson), see my website (www.carolinestrawson.com), or join my free Facebook group, Narcissistic Abuse and Trauma Recovery.

If you're interested in my healing programs and certifications, follow the links below:

- Accredited Narcissistic Trauma Informed Coaching Certification: https://carolinestrawson.com/thehealingcertification

- Healing Codependency: https://carolinestrawson.com/healingcodependency

- Narcissistic Abuse Healing Program: https://www.carolinestrawson.com/nahp

- Narcissistic Abuse Specialist: https://carolinestrawson.com/narcissistic-abuse-specialist

- Regulate: https://carolinestrawson.com/regulate

United States of America

- Allstate Foundation: www.purplepurse.com

- Domestic Violence Legal Empowerment and Appeals Project (DV LEAP): www.nvrdc.org/dv-leap

- Futures Without Violence: www.futureswithoutviolence.org

- Love Is Respect: www.loveisrespect.org

- National Coalition Against Domestic Violence (NCADV): www.ncadv.org

- National Domestic Violence Hotline: www.thehotline.org

- National Network to End Domestic Violence (NNEDV): www.nnedv.org

- RAINN (Rape, Abuse & Incest National Network): www.rainn.org

United Kingdom

- Refuge: www.refuge.org.uk

- Respect: www.respect.uk.net

- Solace: www.solacewomensaid.org

- Women's Aid: www.womensaid.org.uk

Europe

- European Institute for Gender Equality (EIGE): www.eige.europa.eu

- European Women's Lobby: www.womenlobby.org

- Women Against Violence Europe (WAVE): https://wave-network.org/

Canada

- Shelter Safe: www.sheltersafe.ca

- Women's Shelters Canada: www.endvaw.ca

- YWCA Canada: www.ywcacanada.ca

Australia

- 1800RESPECT: www.1800respect.org.au

- Our Watch: www.ourwatch.org.au

- Safe and Equal: https://safeandequal.org.au

- White Ribbon Australia: www.whiteribbon.org.au

REFERENCES

Introduction

1. Seligman, M. E. P. (2011). 'Building human strength: Psychology's forgotten mission.' In: Snyder, et al. *Positive Psychology: The Scientific and Practical Explorations of Human Strengths*. 2nd edition. Thousand Oaks: SAGE Publications, pp. 4–5.

Chapter 1: The Dynamics of Narcissism

1. American Psychiatric Association (2013). *Diagnostic and Statistical Manual of Mental Disorders*. 5th edition. Washington, D.C.: American Psychiatric Association Publishing, Inc.

Chapter 2: Exploring Attachment Styles

1. Bowlby, J. (1958). 'The nature of the child's tie to his mother,' *International Journal of Psycho-Analysis*, 39, pp. 350–73.

2. Ainsworth, M. D. S. and Bell, S. M. (1970). 'Attachment, exploration, and separation: Illustrated by the behavior of one-year-olds in a strange situation,' *Child Development*, 41, pp. 49–67; Bretherton, I. (1992). 'The origins of attachment theory: John Bowlby and Mary Ainsworth,' *Developmental Psychology*, 28(5), pp. 759–75.

3. Schaffer, H. R. and Emerson, P. E. (1964). 'The development of social attachments in infancy,' *Monographs of the Society for Research in Child Development*, 29(3), pp. 1–77.

Chapter 3: It's Not Your Fault

1. Levine, P. A. and Frederick, A. (1997). *Waking the Tiger: Healing Trauma*. Berkeley: North Atlantic Books.

2. Schwartz, R. C. (1995). *Internal Family Systems Therapy*. New York: Guilford Press.

Chapter 4: Understanding the Nervous System

1. Porges, S. W. (2011). *The Polyvagal Theory: Neurophysiological Foundations of Emotions, Attachment, Communication, Self-Regulation*. Norton; Porges, S. W. (2022). 'Polyvagal theory: A science of safety,' *Frontiers in Integrative Neuroscience, 16*, p. 27.

2. Grover, A. and Joshi, A. (2014). 'An overview of chronic disease models: A systematic literature review,' *Global Journal of Health Science, 7*(2), pp. 210–27.

3. Bartlett, S. [Host] (2023, Oct. 12). 'Doctor Gabor Maté: The Shocking link between kindness & illness!' [Video podcast episode.] *The Diary of a CEO*. Retrieved from https://www.youtube.com/watch?v=L7zWT3I3DV0 [Accessed January 26, 2024].

Chapter 6: Moving From Freeze to Thaw

1. Siegel, D. (2017, Aug. 9). 'Dr. Dan Siegel's hand model of the brain.' [Video.] Retrieved from https://www.youtube.com/watch?v=f-m2YcdMdFw&t=2s [Accessed January 26, 2024].

2. *Ibid.*

3. Davis, D. M. and Hayes, J. A. (2012, Jul./Aug.). 'What are the benefits of mindfulness?' American Psychological Association. Retrieved from https://www.apa.org/monitor/2012/07-08/ce-corner [Accessed January 26, 2024].

4. Khoury, B., et al. (2013). 'Mindfulness-based therapy: A comprehensive meta-analysis,' *Clinical Psychology Review, 33*(6), pp. 763–71; Behan, C. (2020); 'The benefits of meditation and mindfulness practices during times of crisis such as COVID-19,' *Irish Journal of Psychological Medicine, 37*(4), pp. 256–8.

5. Hölzel, B.K., et al. (2011). 'Mindfulness practice leads to increases in regional brain gray matter density,' *Psychiatry Research, 191*(1), pp. 36–43;

Tang, R., et al. (2020). 'Brief mindfulness meditation induces gray matter changes in a brain hub,' *Neural Plasticity*, p. 8830005.

6. Levine, P. A. (n.d.). Ergos Institute of Somatic Education. Retrieved from https://www.somaticexperiencing.com [Accessed January 26, 2024].

7. Dana, D. and Porges, S. W. (2018). *The Polyvagal Theory in Therapy: Engaging the Rhythm of Regulation*. New York: W. W. Norton & Co, Inc.

Chapter 7: The Power of Positive Psychology

1. Bolier, L., et al. (2013). 'Positive psychology interventions: A meta-analysis of randomized controlled studies,' *BMC Public Health*, *13*(119); Carr, A., et al. (2020). 'Effectiveness of positive psychology interventions: A systematic review and meta-analysis,' *Journal of Positive Psychology*, *16*(6), pp. 749–69.

2. Neff, K. (2015). *Self-Compassion: Stop Beating Yourself Up and Leave Insecurity Behind*. William Morrow; Neff, K. and Germer, C. K. (2018). *The Mindful Self-Compassion Workbook: A Proven Way to Accept Yourself, Build Inner Strength, and Thrive*. New York: Guilford Press.

3. Hutcherson, C. A., Seppala, E. M., and Gross, J. J. (2008). 'Loving-kindness meditation increases social connectedness,' *Emotion*, *8*(5), pp. 720–4; Kong, F., et al. (2018). 'The relationships among gratitude, self-esteem, social support, and life satisfaction among undergraduate students,' *Journal of Happiness Studies*, *19*(1), pp. 257–68.

4. Via Institute on Character (n.d.). Character strengths. Retrieved from https://www.viacharacter.org/character-strengths-via [Accessed January 26, 2024].

5. Bannink, F. (2012). *Practicing Positive CBT: From Reducing Distress to Building Success*. Hoboken: Wiley-Blackwell.

Chapter 8: Finding Meaning and Purpose in Narcissistic Abuse

1. Seligman, M. (2012). *Flourish: A Visionary New Understanding of Happiness and Well-Being*. New York: Atria.

2. *Ibid.*

Chapter 9: Awakening to Post-Traumatic Growth

1. Tedeschi, R. G. and Calhoun, L. G. (1996), 'The Posttraumatic Growth Inventory: Measuring the positive legacy of trauma,' *Journal of Traumatic*

Stress, 9(3), pp. 455–71; Calhoun, L. G. and Tedeschi, R. G. (2006). 'The foundations of posttraumatic growth: An expanded framework,' In: Calhoun, L. G. and Tedeschi, R. G. (Eds.). *Handbook of Posttraumatic Growth: Research and Practice.* Lawrence Erlbaum Associates, Inc., pp. 3–23.

2. Tedeschi, R. G. and Calhoun, L. G. (1996), 'The Posttraumatic Growth Inventory: Measuring the positive legacy of trauma,' *Journal of Traumatic Stress, 9*(3), pp. 455–71.

Chapter 10: The Story of Your Healing

1. Campbell, J. (1949). *The Hero with a Thousand Faces.* New York: Pantheon Books; Campbell, J. (2014). *The Hero's Journey.* Novato: New World Library.

2. Carrillo, A., et al. (2019). 'Qualitative analysis of the Best Possible Self intervention: Underlying mechanisms that influence its efficacy,' *Plos One, 14*(5), p. e0216896; Padilla, L. M., et al. (2018). 'Decision making with visualizations: A cognitive framework across disciplines,' *Cognitive Research: Principles and Implications, 3*(29).

Chapter 11: Your Best Future Self

1. Maslow, A. H. (1973). 'A theory of human motivation,' In: Lowry, R. J. (Ed.). *Dominance, Self-Esteem, and Self-Actualization: Germinal Papers of H. A. Maslow.* Monterey: Brooks/Cole, pp. 153–73.

2. Hsu, H. P. (2021). 'The psychological meaning of self-forgiveness in a collectivist context and the measure development,' *Psychology Research and Behavior Management, 14*, pp. 2059–69; Davis, D. E., et al. (2015). 'Forgiving the self and physical and mental health correlates: A meta-analytic review,' *Journal of Counseling Psychology, 62*(2), pp. 329–35; Griffin, B. J., et al. (2015). 'Forgiveness and mental health,' in: Toussaint, L. L., Worthington Jr., E. L., and Williams, D. R. (Eds.), *Forgiveness and Health: Scientific Evidence and Theories Relating Forgiveness to Better Health.* New York: Springer Science + Business Media, pp. 77–90.

3. Chowdhury, M. R. (2019, Apr. 9), 'The neuroscience of gratitude and effects on the brain.' PositivePsychology.com. Retrieved from https://positivepsychology.com/neuroscience-of-gratitude/ [Accessed January 26, 2024].

ACKNOWLEDGMENTS

Without my work with Niyc Pidgeon, who has been an amazing mentor and friend to me, I would not have met Kyle Gray. Kyle introduced me to Hay House and the rest, as they say, is history. Thank you to Kezia Bayard-White, Grace Rahman, and Julia Kellaway for all your support.

My children are what drive me to make the world a better place each and every day. William and Madeleine are the most amazing human beings and I love them with all my heart. I'm so proud of them and all they are doing and achieving. When you heal yourself, you really do heal the next generation.

But really this book is in loving memory of my mother, Linda Patricia Hovland. I truly believe the purpose of her death was to give me the gift of healing and to go and help millions of others heal from trauma and abusive relationships. My mother was my rock and, had she been here when I split up from my ex-husband, I would have relied on her as my soft place to fall. I would have been totally dependent on her to rescue me. Yet, her sudden death meant I had no one to rescue me – my father was emotionally unavailable, and my two wonderful sisters lived miles away. My children were totally reliant on me, so I knew I had to rescue myself – for myself and my children. My mother gave me the gift of the life I now live and the space to retrain from being a podiatrist to now help you. She was the most loving mother and I feel her presence all the time, cheering me on to help support you all in rescuing yourselves.

I love you, Mum. Rest in peace.

Photo by Jumarey Mosuela

About the Author

Caroline Strawson is a multi-award-winning somatic trauma therapist, educator, positive psychology coach, and author. She is the host of the number-one iTunes podcast Trauma & Narcissism Redefined, which has over 5 million downloads. She is driven to help others heal and is an expert in narcissism and nervous system regulation.

Caroline is the founder of The Mental Wellbeing Company, which helps individuals, schools, and workplaces enhance mental health and well-being. She teaches the world's only trauma-informed coaching and leadership qualification, CMI level 7, a master's degree equivalent.

Caroline is highly trained in Internal Family Systems, somatic experiencing, brainspotting, EMDR, breathwork, and the Safe and Sound Protocol. She is a clinical hypnotherapist and master trainer, and holds a postgraduate certificate in Applied Positive Psychology and Coaching Psychology.

Caroline freely speaks about her personal experience of domestic abuse and narcissism, and is a self-confessed trauma geek. She has regularly appeared in national and international magazines and newspapers, and on TV and radio, as an expert in her field. She has a huge social media following of over 300,000. She genuinely believes that her own trauma has led her to her true purpose of being a leader, change-maker, and educator in the space of trauma and narcissism.

www.carolinestrawson.com

@carolinestrawson

@carolinestrawson

@CarolineStrawsonHealing

CONNECT WITH
HAY HOUSE
ONLINE

🌐 hayhouse.co.uk   𝐟 @hayhouse

📷 @hayhouseuk   𝕏 @hayhouseuk

▶ @hayhouseuk   ♪ @hayhouseuk

Find out all about our latest books & card decks • Be the first to know about exclusive discounts • Interact with our authors in live broadcasts • Celebrate the cycle of the seasons with us • Watch free videos from your favourite authors • Connect with like-minded souls

'The gateways to wisdom and knowledge are always open.'

Louise Hay